A Greater Good

Also by Robert B. Zevin

The Growth of Manufacturing in
Early Nineteenth Century New England

A Greater Good

Potentials for an Intelligent Economy

Robert B. Zevin

Houghton Mifflin Company · Boston
1983

Library of Congress Cataloging in Publication Data

Zevin, Robert Brooke.
A greater good.

Includes bibliographical references and index.
1. United States—Economic policy—1981–
2. United States—Economic conditions—1945–
3. Inflation (Finance)—United States. I. Title.
HC106.8.Z48   1983   338.973   82-23414
ISBN 0-395-32530-7

Printed in the United States of America

S 10 9 8 7 6 5 4 3 2 1

Acknowledgments

Portions of this book originally appeared in different form in *The Atlantic Monthly* (April and June 1981; and August 1982) and in *Working Papers* (Spring 1975; November/December 1980).

My wife and children have provided me with generous amounts of patience and support at just the time when I had little of either to give to them. I am grateful to Austin Olney of Houghton Mifflin for his gentle encouragement and advice, and to Lois M. Randall of Houghton Mifflin for her thoughtful and acute attention to the broad scope and minor details of the manuscript.

My friends and colleagues Roger Alcaly, Nathan Bossen, and Peter Temin each read portions of the manuscript and did me the great kindness of providing valuable criticisms. My agent, John Brockman, was equally helpful with his time and advice. Another friend, John Case, applied his keen and valuable judgment to the entire manuscript.

I owe a special acknowledgment to Jonathan Weiner, who read numerous drafts of every portion of this book. His comments and suggestions were extraordinarily helpful. His enthusiasm and encouragement were even more valuable.

———————————————

He proceeds to quote passages . . . which
implicitly and explicitly state the principle
that a man who sets before himself a greater
good and then does a lesser, sins.

WATKIN WILLIAMS
Saint Bernard of Clairvaux, 1935

Contents

Introduction

But, soon or late, it is ideas, not vested interests, which
are dangerous for good or evil.

JOHN MAYNARD KEYNES
*The General Theory of Employment,
Interest, and Money* (1936)

This is a book about ideas. Knowledge, education, and ideas are
the strength with which we have transcended material deprivation. By the same token, ignorance and confusion are much
greater threats to our well-being than any shortage of material
investments or resources. In recent years the American electorate has embraced ideas about the economy that are plainly irra-
tional and detached from experience. These notions have
sprung like mushrooms out of the decay of an idea of great
importance: that our individual lives have meaning as part of an
organic society of human beings.

A counterpart to our declining sense of community or of past
or of future is a deterioration in our understanding of the world.
A genuine understanding implies a capacity to relate events to
some predicted consequences. Without understanding, in this
sense, we are unable to determine appropriate actions and policies to achieve desired ends; neither social nor selfish goals can
be intelligently approached.

Understanding is one precondition for action. The other requirement for action is a well-defined set of objectives. We must
know not only the consequences of different actions, but also
which consequences we seek. I have fulfilled this requirement
by using my own social values. The recalcitrant reader who
does not share my premises about what ought to be will nevertheless have an opportunity to observe how my particular tools
of understanding might be employed, just as one might learn

something about hitting a baseball by watching the opposing team at bat, without cheering the results. Regardless of such differences, I hope that everyone will find in these pages reasons for a renewed belief in the future along with increased comprehension of the past and present, and that no one will find these purposes unworthy.

I begin with inflation, because it has been the source or consequence of so much of our distress in recent decades. If inflation has disappeared before these words are read, that sudden disappearance will also be the cause of a serious economic malady. In any case, an examination of inflation is a convenient avenue to a general explanation of how a modern economy functions. We will then look at the very material consequences of the very abstract idea of money. I will show that money, like so many other elements of our economic structure, is a social creation, not some object with an independent existence.

After money, I will explain something more about how an impulse toward inflation or depression can exist in the present for reasons that are predetermined. If we cannot see this clearly, we are destined to be swept back and forth by these tides instead of navigating our own course. Next, we will consider the intellectual origins of the ineffective and incondite policies that have been developed and applied over the past decade. I will show the futility of pursuing a too narrow self-interest in the context of an intricate social organization. I will also explain how economic ideas, like the model of perfect competition, have been perverted from standards for the improvement of reality into false assertions about the essence of reality.

I conclude with some specific methods for ending inflations. And I recapitulate the once well-known strategic principles by which we could (or should) end a depression.

Among the many ideas in this book that are offered, criticized, and chronicled or whose critical relationship to the economy is revealed, one merits special emphasis at the beginning. In addition to the importance of ideas *about* the economy, ideas have now become a primary factor *in* the economy. Ideas themselves are the principal commodity that we produce and consume, store and transport, save and invest in.

PART I

Inflation:
Its Roots
and Fruits

1

Spending Excess Money

Inflation is always and everywhere a monetary
phenomenon.
MILTON FRIEDMAN
"What Price Guideposts?" (1966)

The defining feature of a state of inflation is that prices are
increasing. If all prices are expressed in money, it is a trivial
amendment to say that the *money* prices of things are increasing. It does not follow from this additional adjective that inflation is caused by money in a meaningful sense any more than it
is caused by the passage of time over which prices are rising.
The question remains whether increasing prices are always
caused by increasing money and whether the latter can ever
occur without causing the former.

It is not difficult to understand how the price of one thing
might increase relative to the price of another. A freeze in Florida can make oranges relatively scarce, so that their price increases when compared with the prices of avocados and automobiles. A war might increase the demand for airplanes, with a
consequent increase in the price of titanium or in the salaries of
aeronautical engineers. Inflation is distinct from these phenomena. It involves a more or less simultaneous increase in the
money price of everything.

When money itself was just a commodity, like gold or tobacco, inflation and deflation could still be viewed as special
cases of relative abundance or scarcity. If new gold was discovered in vast quantities, gold became relatively plentiful and
cheap. It took fewer oranges or less tin to purchase the same
ounce of gold. Therefore, it took more ounces of gold to purchase the same quantity of oranges, tin, or anything else. Since

3

gold was money, the money-gold price of everything was increased. There was a general inflation. Conversely, if a blight destroyed most of the tobacco crop in seventeenth-century Virginia, tobacco became a relatively scarce commodity. It took more oranges to obtain the same amount of tobacco. The price of everything in terms of tobacco was decreased, and there was a general deflation.

I shall return in Part II to a history of the growth of money beyond the confines of gold or tobacco. It should be apparent, without further argument at this point, that the abundance or scarcity of money no longer depends on the supply of any substantive commodity. Of course, if money is now produced on printing presses instead of in gold mines, a speeding up of those presses might still have the same effect as the plunder of Incan treasures, by inflating the supply of money and the money prices of everything else at the same time.

Those who call themselves monetarists believe that the speed of the monetary presses is an independent cause of events, while the behavior of the value of incomes and production (Gross National Product, or GNP) and prices and wages (inflation) are all derivatives of the rate at which money is created. There are two propositions concerning money about which there is no fundamental disagreement between monetarists and the rest of us.

First, people and businesses hold money either to be ready to make purchases or as one among many ways of maintaining their saved wealth for use in the future. Except to the extent that some wealth is intended to be held forever and never spent, the distinction between these two motives — spending and saving — is only a matter of an arbitrary time horizon. Most people save part of Friday's paycheck to purchase Tuesday's lunch. Many people save out of every week's pay to finance their Christmas presents. Some people set aside part of every year's earnings for a comfortable retirement. The more distant or unlikely the intended expenditure, the less constraint to hold the corresponding wealth in the form of money rather than as some other asset, like stocks and bonds or real estate.

The second proposition is that the total of these demands to hold money will increase in rough proportion to increases in the quantity of real economic activity and money prices, or approximately in proportion to changes in the dollar value of GNP. This is obviously true in the case of money held to finance immediate transactions: the more numerous and costly the transactions, the more money required to finance them. It is also true of money held as a component of saved assets, to the extent that wealth increases with income and that money is a constant proportion of wealth. These propositions are obviously rough approximations. People who spend all their income and are paid once a week will hold on the average half a week's income in money for transactions. The same people, paid once a month, will hold an average of two weeks' income in money. Such a shift will quadruple the spending demand for money with no change in activity or prices. The savings demand for money will also fluctuate, depending on people's expectations for the economy and the prices of alternative investments.

Monetarism is distinguished by its third proposition: The amount of money supplied to an economy is determined by gold discoveries, the proclivities of central bankers, or some other set of Olympian forces that affect the economy with little necessary regard for the amounts of money it might demand. Then, in the representative words of one monetarist economist, "if the amount of money supplied is greater than the amount that individuals desire to hold, an *excess supply* of money exists. Individuals will attempt to rid themselves of the excess money by increasing their purchases of goods and services." The process continues until it drives activity, prices, or some combination of the two, up to the values at which individuals and businesses will want to hold the increased amount of money that has been supplied.

Whether money is a function of the value of GNP or an independent cause is not so easily established by merely examining the historical records of these two magnitudes. Monetarists are inclined to emphasize the proportionality of this relationship; the rest of us focus on the irregularities. But this misses the point. Both a close and a ragged correspondence are consistent with causation running in either direction, since monetarists and their critics agree on the first two propositions, which imply some degree of correspondence between money and the money value of GNP.

Monetarists have attempted to resolve this difficulty by demonstrating that changes in the quantity of money typically occur sometime before the corresponding changes in the value of total economic activity. Although they have generally succeeded in demonstrating this proposition, the length of time by which wiggles in a graph of money precede wiggles in a graph of GNP varies considerably. Sometimes it seems to disappear altogether (money and GNP fluctuate simultaneously).

But the argument does not founder so much on faulty evidence as it does on abysmal logic. The belief that a temporal sequence necessarily implies a causal sequence is a primitive fallacy. Volcanoes often emit smoke before they erupt with lava. Yet the smoke does not cause the lava flow. Rather, both are consequences of the same subterranean events. The smoke, the lava, and the order of their appearance are all merely symptoms of an unobserved cause.

In the same way, increases in the quantity of money, followed by increases in the money measure of GNP, may also be dual symptoms of some other force that determines the order and the nature of their appearance. Looking at a larger body of evidence provides a clue to one such possibility. While the relationship between the quantity of money and GNP is irregular with regard to both the timing of their respective variations and the proportionality, the relationship between the fraction of GNP that is represented by debt financing and the rate of inflation has been comparatively consistent for a remarkably long time.

(Out of consideration for the sensibilities of readers who blanch at the sight of legions of numbers and their statistical analysis, I have banished an explication of the historical relationships among various definitions of money, borrowing, GNP, and inflation to an appendix to this chapter that is confined to the rear of the book.)

In the next chapter I will offer an explanation for the correlation of borrowing and inflation. We will find that it is more accurate to say that excess spending creates its own money rather than to believe that excess money creates more spending.

2

Financing
Excess Spending

> Money in its significant attributes is, above all, a subtle
> device for linking the present to the future; and we
> cannot even begin to discuss the effect of changing ex-
> pectations on current activities except in monetary
> terms.
>
> JOHN MAYNARD KEYNES
> *The General Theory of Employment,*
> *Interest, and Money* (1936)

Suppose you decide to join the dwindling ranks of those who go
to their friendly neighborhood dealer and purchase a new car.
Every cent that you spend on your purchase can be accounted
for in a quite straightforward way as someone else's income. A
portion of your check may represent a state excise tax, which is
income for the state government. A percentage will become the
salesman's commission — his income. Part of what remains
after the dealer's cost for the car will be used to pay his rent, his
electric bill, and other expenses. Whatever still remains is the
dealer's profit (and therefore his income) or, in the case of a
negative number, his loss (and therefore a subtraction from his
income).

The bulk of your check will represent the money the dealer
has paid the manufacturer for the automobile. But the manufacturer in turn will spend these proceeds on wages, rent, interest,
electricity, and other operating expenses. In addition, the automobile company will have purchased glass and steel and a myriad of items from other producers. What is still left is the automobile company's profit or loss. This in turn becomes the
income of stockholders through dividend payments, the income

8

of governments through tax payments, or the retained income of the automobile company itself. In a similar fashion we can pursue all of the payments made to the landlords, the electric companies, the steel companies or their suppliers, the coal companies, until everything turns into someone's wages or interest or rent or dividend, the tax collected by a government, or the retained profit of a business.

What is true for cars is true equally for butter and postage stamps. The amount paid by the final purchaser creates a like amount of income to be divided among the various recipients in the chain of production: dairy farmers and supermarket clerks, letter carriers and mail truck manufacturers. It follows that the total amount spent on the final purchase of all goods and services in the course of a year is just equal to the total incomes earned in the same year. Hence, the National Income and Product Accounts are so named as a recognition that they reflect, and can be calculated from, these two different aspects of the same process.

So far we have been talking of a mere accounting identity between the total value of production and the total income of the producers. However, it is clear that in our society there is nothing to prevent a particular family or business, let alone a unit of government, from spending more or less than its income in a given year. Indeed, the individual unit that is in perfect balance between income and expenditure is the rare exception among us. If the total of desired purchases falls short of the total income and production, in the short run the identity between production and income is preserved by adhering to the accounting conventions that the manufacturer of unwanted automobiles has purchased them as additions to inventory, while the barber who pays his rent and light bills, but has no customers, is said to enjoy a negative income. With purchases thus redefined upward and income similarly redefined downward, we can demonstrate that the two magnitudes are identical. Before too long, the automobile company will stop producing cars it cannot sell by closing plants and reducing employment. The barber will abandon his shop. Wages, rents, and other kinds of income will fall, and the aggregate willingness to spend will also decline with this drop in total incomes. Eventually these and other events will produce a new equilibrium at which total incomes just equal total desires to spend. This is the analysis of recurrent unemployment and occasionally severe depression that was developed in the 1930s by John Maynard Keynes.

Let us examine the implications of the opposite initial state of affairs. What happens if the total amount that some families and institutions wish to spend beyond their incomes exceeds the total amount by which the spending plans of others falls short of their incomes?

The initial impact will mostly be upon surplus or idle resources. If the demand for automobiles increases, the dealers and manufacturers will be happy to sell out their inventories as well as to market all of their current production. Unemployed barbers and their empty shops will be employed again when the demand for haircuts increases. But what if the economy is already at a reasonably high utilization of its resources? Or what if the specific increases in demand are for skills and products or in places where there is no idle surplus to draw upon?

If the excess demand for goods cannot be satisfied by an increase in domestic production, there is always the chance that it can be met by increasing imports of the desired goods. Both increases in domestic production and increases in imports solve the original problem of spending desires in excess of income only if they cause income to increase faster than spending. The reemployed autoworkers and barbers are going to want to spend more when they have renewed incomes. So too, perhaps, the landlord of the previously vacant barbershop or the beneficiaries of increased dividends on auto company stocks. Similarly, if American imports are increased, the foreign nations that receive more dollars may decide to spend more dollars for American goods. Thus, the original excess of demand would come back home through the increased demand for American exports.

If neither increased production nor increased imports are feasible responses to an original excess of demand over production, increased prices are the remaining possibility. If the excessive spending intentions are budgeted in terms of dollars, then an inflation will effectively ration the available supply of real production to the dollar budgets. In an economy producing its maximum capacity of 100 widgets at $1 apiece, suppose that the aggregate desire to purchase widgets totals $102, although incomes are only $100. If the price of widgets rises to $1.02 (2 percent inflation), then $102 will buy the same 100 widgets. National income will increase from $100 to $102 with the sales value of the widgets, thus restoring the required identity between income and the value of production.

We need to look more closely at how a decision to spend in excess of income is implemented by a particular family, business, or government. We are most familiar with the case of governments. A government that decides to spend more than its revenues from taxes and other sources is said to incur a *deficit* equal to this difference. Such deficits are normally financed by issuing debt (borrowing money). The debt is purchased (money is loaned) by individuals and banks or sometimes by businesses and other units of government. We may think of the individual purchaser as using savings that resulted from a decision to spend less than income. We may think of the banks as sometimes using individuals' savings, which they hold as deposits, and sometimes creating new money by their purchases, as will be explained further in Part II. The purchasing bank will generally not be aware of which procedure it is effecting.

Deficit spending is still more the ordinary state of affairs for businesses than for governments. Even in times of high profits and low inflation, the typical business spends most of its revenues on wages, supplies, and taxes. A good portion of what remains is used to maintain or replace existing buildings and equipment or is paid out as interest and dividends. The balance of retained profit is rarely adequate to finance the purchase of new facilities for the expansion of the business, so the deficits created by such expenditures are financed by the sale of new stocks and bonds or by increased borrowing from banks. Again, the stocks and bonds end up being owned mostly by individuals; the bank loans may represent either the indirect investment of individual saving or the creation of new money.

In contrast, the average household typically saves some portion of its income. However, every year about one out of every forty families decides to buy a new house. Such families are inevitably required to spend more than their incomes in the year of purchase, since the median price of a new house is more than three times the median family income. The resulting deficit is usually financed by drawing on the family's existing pool of savings to pay between a tenth and a quarter of the cost of the house and borrowing the rest in the form of a mortgage. European vacations, college educations for children, and the purchase of new cars are often financed in similar fashion, although the proportion paid from prior savings is higher and that from borrowing is lower.

Some important lessons emerge from all of these examples. In every case, a decision to spend more than current income is implemented by drawing on existing cash balances, selling existing securities, issuing new securities, or borrowing from a bank. Drawing on cash balances converts money that had been idle as a store of value into money that is active as a means of payment. If a family sells its government bonds or corporate bonds and stocks to another family that draws on its savings to pay for these securities, the effect is exactly the same. This shift of some portion of the stock of money from a passive to an active role is a possibility with which economists are familiar. They call it an increase in the *velocity* of money. The same quantity of money becomes consistent with a higher value of GNP. In the inflation from the end of World War II through the early 1980s, GNP did increase faster than the quantity of money, no matter how money is defined (see the Appendix). That is, the velocity of money increased.

If deficits are financed by issuing new securities or by borrowing from banks, this is likely to contribute both to an increase in velocity and to an increase in money. The velocity effect is the same as that just described. If households deplete their cash balances, representing accumulated savings, in order to purchase the new securities issued by governments or corporations, the households presumably believe that the new securities are a superior way to hold savings; but the money that had been passive in the household account is put to active use by the borrowing government or corporation. If corporate and government deficits are financed by bank purchases of the new securities or by direct bank lending, these activities will lead to some amount of new money creation.

Another set of lessons should be noted now, for future reference and to clarify what has already been said. Deficit spending is sometimes forced on a family, business, or government by desperate circumstances, meaning an income that is inadequate compared to perceived necessities. Sometimes it is also chosen by the profligate or the irresponsible. Our political system encourages such spendthrift traits in government policymakers. However, for the most part, deficit spending is justified by the purchase of an asset that is durable.

Houses and automobiles, commercial buildings and industrial machines, highways and nuclear aircraft carriers, overseas travel and college educations are all durable in the sense that they will provide some satisfaction, service, or revenue for a length of time into the future without having to be replaced. The family that buys a house commits itself to a series of future mortgage payments coincident with its future occupancy of the house. The debt issued to pay for the construction of a new school will be serviced by future levies of school taxes over the decades in which subsequent generations of students use the building.

A final lesson is this. Borrowing carries a commitment to future saving. A portion of future school tax levies must be used not to construct additional schools or hire new teachers, but to retire the existing debt. Similarly, a portion of every monthly mortgage payment represents a reduction of the homeowner's debt and therefore contributes to the eventual completion of the purchase. Consequently, most individuals are either saving directly to make down payments on cars and houses or saving indirectly through monthly payments on existing auto loans and mortgages. Only a small minority are dissaving by borrowing to complete a current purchase.

My concern in this discussion is with the possibility that decisions to spend more than income might overwhelm decisions to spend less than income, rather than with the forces that tend to keep the two in approximate balance. It should be clear from what has already been said that an excess of spending over income will lead to increases in both the quantity and the velocity of money, along with the value of GNP. If the new demand is focused on surplus resources, these will be employed and sold with a consequent increase in real GNP. But if that demand is for production that cannot be readily increased, GNP will grow only as a result of price inflation.

An increase in the deficits of excess spenders compared with the surpluses of savers necessarily implies an increase in total borrowing and sales of securities. These activities, in turn, imply some increase in the quantity of money. Since money must be raised before it can be spent, this excess of spending desires will lead to the creation of new money before it is manifest as an increase in effective demand. Moreover, the initial increase in demand will ramify as it creates new incomes, which lead to new demands that create still more incomes. Accordingly, the full increase in the value of GNP, whether it be in the form of greater output or inflation, will usually be observed some time after the initial increase in the quantity of money. Both the increase in money and the subsequent increase in the value of economic activity will be caused by the initial excess of desired spending over available income at current levels of output and prices.

Thus a given amount of money is compatible with different levels of spending, depending on how much money is hoarded and spent and how rapidly the latter portion changes hands. By contrast, a given amount of spending will finance itself through increases in both the velocity and the quantity of money. The proximate cause of inflation is not too much *money* so much as too much *spending*. In any growing economy, some units and sectors will borrow what others have saved. If, for whatever reasons, desires to borrow and spend exceed desires to save and lend, the relative magnitude of borrowing will increase and either the prices or the quantities of economic activity will grow in proportion.

In the next four chapters I shall consider some of the factors that have encouraged an inflationary tendency toward excessive borrowing and spending over the past three or four decades. In sequence, we will look at the effects of Keynesian management, at long swings in the course of industrial innovation and maturation, at oil prices, and at inflation itself, as roots of inflation.

3

The Failure
of Success

There remains the problem of keeping the economy
from straying too far above or below the path of steady
high employment. One way lies inflation, and the other
way lies recession. Flexible and vigilant fiscal and monetary policies will allow us to hold the narrow middle
course.

JOHN F. KENNEDY
The Economic Report of the President (1962)

As noted in the last chapter, the Keynesian analysis of unemployment and depression is just the analysis of inflation in
reverse. If the total of the spending intentions of people, businesses, and governments is less than the total of their prospective incomes, the result will be a decline in production and incomes until the excess of income over desired spending is
eliminated. This decline, like the increase occasioned by the
opposite imbalance, occurs partly in real employment and output and partly in prices and wages. Ever since the Great Depression, governments in Western Europe, North America, and
Japan have acted on their belief in this analysis.

If unmanaged demand falls short of high employment production because of some undulation in the age distribution of
the population, the tendency of businesses to move in herds
from optimistic new construction to pessimistic restraint, or
even some vagaries of the weather, then clearly the social loss
and individual misery of unemployment can be eradicated by
inducing or producing the missing component of spending required to make demand equal to high employment supply.
Keynes argued that governments have the ability to induce

16

more private spending by making loans readily available. If such efforts still failed to encourage private spending commensurate with prosperity, the government itself could always increase its own spending as much beyond its income as the private sector failed to spend out of its high employment income. In such a case the government could borrow the difference out of the surplus saving of individuals or businesses. Thus a government dedicated to sustaining production and employment will indirectly encourage or directly create what Keynes called "loan-expenditures" in his 1933 pamphlet, *The Means to Prosperity*.

Adherence to these policies in all industrial democracies produced spectacular results for the first two decades after World War II. Business fluctuations did not disappear; but economic contractions were shorter and shallower, and average unemployment was lower than had been the case for any comparable interval since the Industrial Revolution in the eighteenth century. At first, economic decision makers were skeptical of both the permanence and the efficacy of these new policies. Increasingly, the eloquence of events persuaded people that many unpleasant possibilities had been banished from the post-Keynesian world.

Growing confidence produced a growing willingness to spend and to finance more spending with more borrowing. In the 1930s, and in earlier depressions, when jobs were lost or wages declined many people found it impossible to continue payments on auto loans or home mortgages. A business that had gone into debt to expand capacity was equally distressed by a contraction of demand. Even state and local governments had been forced to default on their obligations. Since prices fell with employment, it was often not possible to raise enough money by selling a house or factory to repay the debt that had financed it, let alone obtain money for other urgent needs. Depressions were bad times to be in debt. And they were good times to have a nest egg of savings, so that one could keep creditors from foreclosing and continue to eat. Thus, if depressions had been abolished, an important restraint on borrowing and an inducement to saving had been abolished along with them.

To the extent that people believed that the Keynesian state stood ready to borrow and to spend whatever they collectively saved, they tended to spend more and save less, thus obviating the need for the state actually to deliver on its promise. At this level of generality, success was not a problem. As every Keynesian textbook explained, the government's role was to balance the economy at high employment by offsetting either an excess or a shortfall of saving. If other units were willing to spend more of their incomes, the government could simply spend less. If euphoria over permanent success led to a collective willingness constantly to borrow and spend more than total incomes, the inflationary consequences could be forestalled by having the government constantly raise more taxes than it spent.

If we look at the postwar economy's movements from year to year, it is apparent that its structure, especially the design of federal fiscal policy, did tend to restrain divergences toward inflation as well as recession. When new spending causes a sudden increase in GNP, a disproportionate part of that increase tends to become the additional income of corporations. If the new spending leads to higher prices, there is a tendency for the selling prices of products to increase sooner or further than wages, rents, and other corporate expenses. The result is a swelling of profits. If the spending leads instead to increased output, the effect on profits is still the same. The new production by businesses tends to be more profitable than prior production, because it does not require proportionate increases in labor, buildings, and machinery. Thus, while corporate profits after-tax averaged about 5 percent of GNP in the 1950s and 1960s, their increase over the first year or two of cyclical expansions was about 20 percent of any increase in GNP.

Corporations are slow to change their dividend policies or their rates of spending on new capital. Therefore, when GNP increased by $10 billion, more than $2 billion became increased corporate profits and was effectively stopped cold before it could again become someone else's income or a demand for someone else's product. Corporate profits tend to cushion a decline in GNP in exactly the same way. When spending falls unexpectedly, over 20 percent of the consequent reduction of incomes appears as a decline in the after-tax profits of corporations. Again, corporate dividends and capital spending change belatedly. For a while, at least, 20 percent of the initial drop in spending is absorbed by corporations without being retransmitted in the form of another round of reduced incomes.

This tendency of profits to serve as cyclical shock absorbers, up and down, was not, of course, a consequence of government policy. It had been true long before World War II, and it remains true today. A unique — and in retrospect, an admirable — feature of the halcyon days between Korea and Vietnam was the impact of government taxes and spending on surges and lapses in spending. Because of progressive income taxes and other features, including the tax on corporate profits, fully a third of short-term variations were absorbed by increased taxes (in the case of increased spending and income) or decreased taxes (in the case of a recession). Like corporations, the federal and local governments are slow to change their spending. However, unemployment compensation and other components of the payments to individuals introduced with the New Deal did change in a swift and peculiar way. They went *down* when incomes and employment increased and they went *up* when GNP declined.

As a result of these tax and transfer-payment effects combined, when spending increased there was an immediate shift by the government sector toward a reduced deficit or increased surplus equal to three eighths of the entire increment to spending, or an equal countervailing movement in the case of a fall in spending. These effects were aptly named "automatic stabilizers." In combination, the government and corporate sectors neutralized almost 60 percent of the destabilizing force of economic swerves in either direction. It is not surprising that short-run impulses *around the longer trend* were quickly stalled and reversed.

However, if the source of increased spending persisted for much more than a year, these stabilizers lost their strength. After a while, corporations adjust to higher incomes and spend them on increased dividends or enlarged capital budgets. A consistent enlargement of profits might make new investment look so attractive that corporations spend *more* than the entire increase on new investment. In similar fashion, it doesn't take very long for the electorate and government officials to respond to improved budget conditions by finding new ways to spend money or reduce taxes.

In fact, inflation has been the nearly constant companion of modern economic management in all the industrial democracies ever since recovery from the Great Depression began in the 1930s. Until the mid-1960s, peacetime rates of price increase were modest but dogged in the United States and many other countries. In recent years, the moderate inflation of the Eisenhower and Kennedy eras has looked like unobtainable perfection. At that time, however, it was widely deplored as an evil in its own right and a symptom of the failure of government policies. To appreciate this failure we must examine more closely the origin and implementation of economic stabilization policies.

The Depression, which these policies were designed to vanquish eternally, was characterized by declines in prices equal to the sickening fall in employment and output. For contemporaries the two processes were inseparable. Fifty years later, their logical connection still seems powerful. Hence, from the beginning, the theory and practice of maintaining prosperity was also a theory and practice of maintaining prices. In *The Means to Prosperity,* Keynes accepts raising prices as a goal equivalent in merit to increasing employment. He argues that both worthy objectives can best be achieved with the single policy of expanding loan-expenditures.

The modern democratic state, committed to maintaining employment and re-electing its own, is committed thereby not only to sustaining the level of total spending, but to sustaining the value of specific prices upon which incomes are dependent. This is especially the case if the prices or incomes affect politically potent groups. Thus the American national government promulgates a minimum wage and stands ready to support the level of many agricultural prices by purchase or by restricting production. It is quite apparent that Lord Keynes opposed most of these devices in principle and many of them in specific detail. For this reason and the fact that some of them originated one hundred years ago, they should not really be called Keynesian.

From the middle of the twentieth century we have had a Keynesian system of income maintenance, whose leanest essentials moved us toward inflation unless they were sternly reduced and reversed in response to the growth of private spending that they fostered. This required policymakers as fearful of inflation as they were of unemployment. However, such serene neutrality was unlikely, given that the unemployed and those fearful of joining them were apt to throw the rascals out, while the recipients of modestly, if meaninglessly, higher money wages and prices were usually quite satisfied with their circumstances. This was a profound source of our inflation.

Programs that provided direct support for incomes and prices through statutory edicts, transfer payments, and regulatory subventions have often been superfluous to maintaining high employment. The nature or magnitude of such programs thus became additional roots of inflation, the programs always being subject to pressure for aggressive application that would raise prices rather than just support them. In part, this aggressiveness was seen as a valuable line of defense against the recurrence of depression; in part, as a more precise policy for improving the relative position of the disadvantaged; and in part, as politically smart, or necessary, since the specificity of the programs made them more measurable and important to particular interest groups. Even without biases and political pressures, this was a system that generally prevented prices from falling but only infrequently kept them from rising. Inevitably such a system will generate a preponderance of price increases. And so it did.

Most of us possess a sound instinct that finds truth in a simple idea over a more complex one. All of us find simplicity easier to comprehend. Keynes's *The General Theory of Employment, Interest, and Money* appeared in 1936 and was immediately subjected to a process of simplification by the economics profession. The simplification took two major directions. One, already implicit in Keynes, is usually present in all economics. For many purposes it is convenient to ignore the obvious fact that people differ in their strength, age, intelligence, education, and inclination or that most machines and buildings are not of identical quality. These simplifications result in the often harmless aggregations of abstract Labor and Capital.

The second simplification was notably absent from Keynes's own explication. In economics, as Keynes repeatedly observed, everything affects everything. Thus, the amount that is spent upon consumption depends not only on the current income of consumers but also upon their habits, as measured by previous consumption and income, their wealth out of which they can also finance purchases, the ease and expense of borrowing, and such specifics as the proportions of people who are in retirement, are close to retirement, are young with many children, and so on. The wealth of consumers depends in part on the value of houses and the level of stock market prices. And each of these in turn has something to do with interest rates, savings behavior, the level of investment, and many other factors. Models of the contemporary American economy, in the Keynesian tradition, often contain over a hundred different economic variables, which appear in as many different equations. All of the variables are determined together, by solving all of the equations simultaneously.

Perhaps with good reason, such a complicated network was considered too difficult for most people to understand. This concern, along with a popular conviction among economists that even a prose as lucid and learned as Keynes's was somehow lugubrious and unscientific compared to completely mathematical statements, produced a drastic simplification similar to our discussion in the previous chapter. Concepts were arranged in sequence, so that each item was the primary factor explaining the next. Thus the level of desired private spending determined whether income would be stable at high employment, would decline, or would be stretched by price inflation. Government spending compared to taxes could compound or compensate any such deviation. The total of these effects would determine whether the economy experienced unemployment, inflation, or the golden mean of full employment with stable prices.

The merits of this system were that it could be understood by undergraduate economics students and by their professors; after a while, it could even be understood by congressmen and Presidents. The elaboration and acceptance of Keynesian policy prescriptions owe much to the power of these simple images. But so does the inflationary outcome of their application. In reality, even at its zenith, modern economic management did not quite achieve the results that this simple theory suggested were possible. There was always some unemployment, even after allowances for the way in which it was measured. At the same time, there was always some inflation.

The mutual persistence of these blemishes was not possible, according to the idealized reduction of economic principles that had been successfully ingrained in popular thought. If demand were inadequate there would be unemployment. If demand were excessive there would be inflation. To experience inflation and unemployment at the same time was a paradox. Economists were quick to seek the answers to this puzzle. Aside from the ingenious and often correct arguments that inflation, unemployment, or both had been mismeasured, the explanations offered by economists fell into two broad categories.

One sort of explanation pointed at monopolies and other concentrations of economic power that thwarted the results that perfect competition would have produced. It followed from this argument that the persistence of unemployment was evidence that aggregate demand and therefore government spending were insufficient; while the persistence of inflation reflected peculiarities in the distribution of economic power that should be addressed by different instruments, such as antitrust policy.

The second type of explanation focused on the distinct peculiarities that occurred among the items that were lumped together as Labor, Capital, or Government Spending. An increased demand for schoolteachers in California might push the salaries of teachers sharply higher without having any impact on the unemployed in West Virginia or New York, unless those places contained unemployed schoolteachers. If, in fact, the demand for schoolteachers was great everywhere, then their salaries would have to stay high long enough for new school-teachers to appear. Some time must elapse before the relatively high earnings of teachers would induce more young adults to enter the labor force with the education and specific training required of a teacher. Even then, this analysis suggested that the ability to acquire these skills successfully depended on the aspirant's wealth, cultural environment, and the quality of his or her schooling. Therefore, while the inflation of teachers' salaries might persist for a long time, very little of the eventual impact on new employment would be felt in those social and geographic segments where unemployment had been highest to begin with.

Neither of these arguments had been unfamiliar to Keynes, who observed clearly and repeatedly that "resources are not homogeneous," and "some commodities will reach a condition of inelastic supply whilst there are still unemployed resources available for the production of other commodities," and that wages "will tend to rise, before full employment has been reached," all of which and more suggested that an "increase in effective demand will, generally speaking, spend itself partly in increasing the quantity of employment and partly in raising the level of prices." For Keynes, the peculiarity of individual resources and commodities, along with the manifest absence of perfect competition in many markets, were both only specific examples of an even more general failure of the actual economy to exhibit the perfectly competitive, highly informative, and effectively motivating price behavior that was imagined in classical economic theory and that could be shown to produce full employment and efficient allocation of effort if only it existed.

Both analyses of the paradox of inflation coincident with unemployment have obvious merits. It is transparent that a large number of businesses and unions possess extraordinary power to set prices according to their assessment of the market rather than just respond to prices as given by the market. Even the local convenience store, if it happens to be the only store within walking distance for you and many of your neighbors, has the power to charge what the traffic will bear rather than having to match the prices that might be set by thousands of more distant competitors. At the national level, a number of basic industries, such as steel, autos, electric appliances, and numerous categories of machinery, are dominated by one or a handful of component firms that have considerable ability to administer their prices. Indeed, it was the perverse practice of the steel industry to raise its prices in the face of falling demand that brought this analysis to prominence in the first place. It was a significant reality that those industries that were dominated by a few powerful firms were also the industries dominated by powerful labor unions.

The market-power analysis of inflation in the face of continuing unemployment raised more profound issues than its proponents may have appreciated. No matter how one measures it, the concentration of market power has not been greater since the end of World War II than it was before. Yet it is undeniable that prices have shown a greater tendency to rise in the face of unemployed resources during the recent period than they did in earlier times. Two aspects of the more recent period are unique. The market power of businesses has been reinforced by the market power of industry-wide unions. The inflationary bias of market imperfections has been reinforced by the consistent application of a Keynesian commitment to high employment.

For one branch of welfare state theorists, it was natural to view the constancy of business power as an immutably inconvenient fact of life and the emergence of union power as an equitable counterbalance to corporate power. For those who held this view, it appeared increasingly obvious that government spending should be increased to assure full employment, while extraordinary government powers should be employed to constrain the inflationary impact of monopoly powers, which produced inflation prematurely and which muffled the impact of employment-expanding expenditures by translating them into increases in prices and monopoly profits rather than in output and employment. The most sweeping and effective way for the government to respond to the price-increasing tendencies of monopolies was for the government to directly regulate the prices charged by monopolies and everyone else. It was thus not an accident that the wage and price controls introduced in 1971 by Richard Nixon were met with widespread approval from Keynesians, including the dean of American disciples, Abba Lerner. Nor is it surprising that Richard Nixon accompanied his introduction of these direct controls by proclaiming that "We are all Keynesians now."

It is fair to say that those who discerned the primary problem in the specific characteristics of the unemployed, or alternatively in the specific demand effects of government expenditures, experienced the zenith of their influence in the epoch of the 1960s under President Kennedy and the earliest days of President Johnson. The original War on Poverty programs contained many specifics designed to pole-vault over the barriers to full employment. Many of the new programs provided "Head Starts" for ghetto children or Job Training for the chronically unemployed or information about job vacancies in one region for the unemployed in another. These solutions were clearly and squarely aimed at a legitimate problem. At the same time, a number of people, including me, believed that job training and similar programs were nothing but sugar coating for a straightforward transfer of income to those who could not obtain jobs with or without additional training.

The rationale for such payments had been provided in the most thoughtful book of the Keynesian nirvana, *The Affluent Society* by John Kenneth Galbraith. We had, argued Galbraith, solved the fundamental problem to which the arguments of all previous economics were addressed: We were without question able to provide every single person with an adequate standard of material comfort. Indeed, the new problem was that we could do all of this without needing to employ everyone who might be eager to work. One solution to this problem was to provide more regular and generous government income payments to those without work or wealth. More production only meant more material gadgets for which demand was created by advertising. Our true requirement was to achieve the universal aristocracy of refinement and reflection which our capacity for universal affluence invited. An essential interim step was to make being unemployed less disreputable and uncomfortable compared to having a job.

At least until the 1980s in the United States (and only shortly before in such hapless places as the United Kingdom) the dominant priority of Keynesian states had been the eradication of unemployment through maintenance of high levels of economic activity. The general improvement created by these policies released inflationary forces that could have been nullified only by a rapid readjustment of the stimulus provided by the state. Since there was always some remaining unemployment, the Keynesian state was encouraged instead to enlarge the policies that had made the initial progress against joblessness.

All the while, inflation was becoming a more active and persistent feature of economic life. Those who attributed the inflation to sectors of the economy that were dominated by powerful firms were inclined to favor direct controls over at least the prices and wages that were not determined in a competitive setting. In this way the inflation could be muzzled and kept from interfering with the continuing fight against unemployment. Those who attributed the inflation to the possibility that some commodities or types of labor could be in short supply while others were unemployed supported efforts to calibrate the composition of the state's fiscal stimulus to more nearly fit the supply of underemployed resources. They also favored specific programs to train, relocate, or otherwise transform the surplus workers and machines into scarce ones.

Both schools agreed on the fundamental proposition that the inflation should in no way be construed as a warning that the drive against unemployment had produced some kind of dangerous overheating. Neither group wanted to admit that the mere success of Keynesian policy coupled with a proper caution toward renewed depression were by themselves sufficient to produce inflation. Nor did the liberals of the 1950s and 1960s choose to place much emphasis on the specific price-propping activities in which the state had become involved.

All of these ideas were applied with varying intensities and durations. Judged on their own terms, it is perhaps not a matter of great consequence that they failed to reverse the acceleration of inflation. However, it is a shortcoming of enormous importance that the continued expansion of Keynesian stimulus, in the form of larger budgets and deficits, also failed to make any additional progress against unemployment after the late 1960s. Since then, unemployment and inflation have not only coexisted; they have increased together. This seems so much at variance with the simplified version of Keynes's thought and the associated explanations of inflation that it has essentially destroyed the faith of voters and officials in the logic of the argument.

In the next chapter we will see how the long sweep of technical change and economic development may have brought us to a particular passage that evokes these twin evils simultaneously. Then we will see how the OPEC price increases also increased unemployment and inflation in tandem.

4

Artificial Respiration

The United States, in the middle of the twentieth century, found itself in a critical situation requiring the urgent attention of thoughtful citizens.

As a nation we had progressed in our domestic development to an extent hardly imaginable a few short decades ago. Internationally, we had emerged as the strongest nation and the best hope of freedom in an explosive world.

Yet, our achievements and our strengths, because of their very magnitude, appeared in some ways to have outrun our goals. There was more than paradox, there was peril in such a situation. A nation which does not shape events through its own sense of purpose eventually will be engulfed in events shaped by others.

LAURANCE S. ROCKEFELLER
on behalf of the
Rockefeller Brothers Fund Trustees (1960)

The commitment of national governments to prevent another depression, which has been unflagging until the recent past, inexorably led to inflation. Legislated price controls and the monopoly power of private interests can account for the fact that particular prices are higher than they otherwise might be. However, a continual increase in prices can be accounted for only by a persistence of excess demand financed with continuous fresh borrowing. The data on the sources of this borrowing strongly suggest that the proximate cause of inflation has been the strengthening of private confidence engendered by Keynesian success far more than the profligate borrowing and spending of Washington bureaucrats.

At the end of World War II, the outstanding debt of the federal government represented 118 percent of a full year's GNP.

29

This proportion fell steadily as GNP expanded from real growth and inflation with little or no help from increasing federal indebtedness. By the middle of the 1970s, the debt of the U.S. government was less than 25 percent of GNP. It has since increased to about 33 percent, which is still less than it was in the 1950s and 1960s. At the same time, business debts have grown more than twice as much as GNP, and the debts of families and individuals (mostly mortgages) have expanded over three times as much as GNP. Put differently, in 1945 federal debt was more than double the debt of businesses and households. Today, the latter groups are in debt for more than three times the obligations of the national government.

At first, private borrowing was encouraged by the reduced fear of depressions, as already explained. In more recent times, borrowing has been provoked by inflation itself, a phenomenon to be examined in chapter 6. During an interim period, from around 1960 through the late 1970s, the magnitude of increased borrowing by businesses substantially exceeded the corresponding numbers for households and the federal government. Much of this business borrowing was motivated by somewhat different concerns, although confidence in Keynesian policies and the benefits that borrowers could gain from inflation also supported the surge of corporate deficit spending.

Because the splurge of corporate excess spending coincided with the period of dramatic escalation in inflation, this chapter offers a more detailed examination of the reasons for this episode of substantial corporate deficits. In brief, the story goes something like this. Around the time that Kennedy succeeded Eisenhower as President, a number of major American industries arrived, more or less simultaneously, at points of market saturation, sharp growth slowdowns, exhaustion of possibilities for technical progress, or some combination of these. As a result, growth became less spontaneous and profit margins shrank. The affected corporations sought to maintain their expected growth rates by investing in new businesses, new techniques, or new parts of the world. Since the return on these investments was low, in the absence of continuing technical progress and prime markets, the required investment increased just when the flow of investable profits was falling. As a consequence, these corporations found it necessary to finance a growing proportion of their investments with borrowed money.

The story is important because the industries involved were among the largest in the United States. Collectively they accounted for a large majority of employment, profits, and the value of capital. The reasons for this coincident slowdown are not accidental. To some extent *every* industry was affected by the maturation of the postwar boom. The Great Depression and World War II had postponed marriage and childbirth as well as many expenditures for houses, durables, and educations. At the same time, at least during the war, many families had accumulated cash balances, government bonds, and other savings that could be spent for these purposes. But by the late 1950s these effects had worn off. The boom in marriages, births, and new suburban houses was over.

Furthermore, the interrelated technologies, which had dominated development since 1900, were reaching the end of their collective rope. It always seems flippant to characterize a matrix of codeveloping technologies with a few unique qualities. Nevertheless, analysis does suggest that the affected industries were related and their problems were similar. Nineteenth century technology involved coal-fired steam engines for transport and industry, and the manufacture of iron, steel, and basic chemicals. Many of these remained important in the twentieth century, but the new technologies increasingly involved internal-combustion engines, burning oil, consumption of petrochemicals, central generation of electricity, and electricity-consuming machines and appliances. Put differently, the new technology gave us the automobile and airplane, suburbia, shopping centers, drive-ins, nylons, washing machines, and TV as the characteristic features of a new age. Just listing these salients suggests a fortress since abandoned.

About twenty years ago, the industries that had pioneered these twentieth century developments approached simultaneous senility. The concurrence of this exhaustion was in part accidental, but in large part it resulted from the interdependence of these products. It was natural that the nation became saturated with highways at the same time that it became saturated with automobiles, leaving both roadbuilders and automakers with the lesser task of maintaining the existing stock rather than contributing to its continuing rapid increase. Naturally as well, the demand for trucks and washing machines, construction equipment and refrigerators, asphalt and coffee tables also was leveled by the maturation of the auto-highway–based development of suburbia.

One might have thought that these developments would also crimp the growth of demand for oil and especially for the electricity that illuminated suburban buildings and powered the appliances that filled the buildings and the factories that made the appliances. However, consumption of oil and electricity soared from the early 1960s to the early 1970s, contributing to the illusions and imbalances that then caused much mischief. In part, this anomalous growth of energy consumption may have been due to the energy-intensive character of the military force that was expanded from the beginning of the Kennedy administration and actively deployed to an increasing extent. In part, the accelerated consumption of energy may have indicated that many optimal uses of oil energy and electricity remained to be exploited. In the early 1960s there were demonstrable opportunities to increase the value of agricultural production with greater use of fertilizers. Production of these fertilizers typically consumed large quantities of natural gas or petroleum. In the steel industry, electric-arc furnaces were still novelties with powerful competitive advantages.

However, the overriding reason that energy consumption spurted as related industries tired is simply a matter of price. The Seven Sisters (five American and two European oil companies that dominated the world market until the OPEC actions of 1973) had achieved a major position for oil at the expense of coal, by maintaining a relatively low and constant price, albeit a very profitable one. As other prices began to rise more rapidly, the oil industry persisted in its previous policy. This is only one among numerous examples of how the existence of strong market power to set prices is likely to contribute to price stability rather than inflation, in the absence of excess demand. From

1960 to 1970, while the general level of American prices rose by 30 percent, the price of crude oil was essentially unchanged.

The electric power industry is a closely related story of mis-regulated monopolies. For about the first eighty years of its history, the central generation and distribution of electricity enjoyed enormous economies of scale. Every time a utility constructed an even larger plant, it was found that given amounts of capital or labor or fuel could generate even greater amounts of electricity. It was to everyone's advantage to encourage increased consumption and production of electricity. As demand grew, bigger new plants were constructed, which lowered the cost of electricity for existing consumers. Electric rate structures reflected this fact by offering increasing price discounts to those who used the most and price incentives to those who added electric heat or hot water to their homes or located new factories in particular utility districts. In the early 1960s, new power plants attained an average size at which these economies were no longer being realized. In particular, it was clear after the first dozen had been completed that nuclear plants were a very high-cost source of new power.

It would be excessively gracious to say that the industry and its regulators were slow to adapt to this new reality. As late as 1977, when President Carter proposed national legislation to eliminate declining rates for increased consumption and to impose penalty rates for consumption during periods of peak demand, the industry responded with an instantaneous invasion of Washington. These proposals were permanently excised from the Carter Energy Program within minutes of the opening of congressional committee hearings on the bill. Even now, twenty years after they became out of date, most utilities have neither changed nor been required to change their outmoded rate schedules.

The result was that consumption and production continued to rapidly outpace GNP until sometime after the first OPEC price shock. From 1960 to 1970, the average price paid for a kilowatt hour actually declined a bit in the face of accelerating inflation elsewhere and deteriorating efficiency for the industry. The result of the industry's stubborn fight to maintain its antiquated rates and to build nuclear plants has been a terrible fall from its former level of secure profitability to its present status as a risky business with poor profits. This story is also an example of how noncompetitive businesses and inert government regulators can contribute to price stability for a long period before reaping the inflationary consequences of their mistakes or yielding to inflationary pressures that originate elsewhere.

If major businesses experienced and expected reduced growth of demand for their products and/or reduced profitability beginning twenty years ago, it is something of a paradox that this caused them to spend more on investment rather than less. The specifics of each case often answer the question. If the growth of domestic demand was slowing down, why not go overseas? American companies did, in growing numbers and with more dollars. If a traditional line of business was slow, why not create or buy a new line with more promise? This, too, happened with bewildering profusion. Oil companies went into the chemical business and vice versa. Pharmaceutical houses added cosmetics and vice versa. Railroad equipment companies went into electronics and elevator manufacturers into oil-field equipment.

The remedy for corporate fatigue was money spent on new plant and equipment in new businesses or in new countries. In this way a firm could maintain its position in the Fortune 500. An executive could maintain his reputation for perspicacity, his bonus, and his job. Electric utilities added a unique and important fillip to this process. From 1960 to 1974 their output and capacity grew nearly twice as fast as real GNP. The real resources required to build this capacity were disproportionately larger because of the exhaustion of economies of scale and the heavy capital requirements of nuclear power. The financial resources were greater still as the investment boom raised the price of capital goods and the interest on borrowed money even more than the general inflation. Electric utilities accounted for a significant and growing fraction of capital spending, nearly one fifth of the total by 1974.

These impulses resulted in the greatest — and least-recognized — capital spending splurge of the twentieth century.

From 1965 through 1974, real business spending for inventories, buildings, and machines averaged 10.6 percent of GNP, which is higher than any other ten-year period since World War I. At the same time, the money that businesses had available for investment from their operations was falling steadily from 10.6 percent of GNP in 1965 to 7 percent in 1974. Therefore, increasing portions of the cost of business spending for new investment had to be paid for with bank borrowing or the sale of new securities. In 1965, these sources of funds accounted for about one third of capital spending, as they had for the previous two decades. In 1974, borrowed money and proceeds from issues of new securities equaled 60 percent of investment expenditures. Subsequently, the external financing of investment has hovered between 40 percent and 50 percent.

This was the decade in which inflation grew to serious proportions. The increase was persistent, from 2.2 percent in 1965 to 8.7 percent in 1974. The average was about 5 percent a year for the entire ten years. Then and now, superficial wisdom looked to the war in Southeast Asia as a prime culprit. Secondary blame was placed on the impact of the new programs of the War on Poverty and the Great Society. If these explanations did not entirely satisfy the doubts of the expositor or the audience, an appeal was made to the inability to supply the economy's demands because of inadequate capacity. The cause of inadequate capacity was alleged to be previous inadequate investment. This was an especially popular argument with businessmen, who claimed that the way to encourage investment (and therefore to cure inflation) was by making public policy more favorable to the earning of large profits.

Most of these propositions turn reality upside-down. Between 1965 and 1974 military expenditures increased by 56 percent while the value of GNP and Gross Private Domestic Investment each increased by more than 100 percent. In fact, the increase in private investment spending was almost equal to the combined increase in both defense spending and transfer payments by the federal government to individuals, which is a fair measure of the economic impact of the Great Society programs. Of more importance, as explained in chapter 2, is the relation of increased spending to available income. Much has been made of the failure of the Johnson administration to seek the tax increases required to pay for the war in Southeast Asia. While there is some validity to this point, it is insignificant compared to the deficits incurred by corporations to finance their investment spree. From 1965 to 1974 the outstanding debt of corporations increased by over one trillion dollars, or more than four times as much as the debt of the federal government and its agencies. The latter increased by less than GNP while corporate debt increased by twice as much.

As for inadequate investment, we have already seen that investment was at record high levels. The pressure of production on capacity was greater in both 1965 and 1966 than it has been in any year since. The investment spree produced a growing margin of surplus capacity. Inflation did not result from too little investment but from too much. That new investment went to expensive and inefficient facilities, like nuclear power plants, or to redundant facilities in somebody else's business, only compounded the inflation. An additional piece of evidence for the proposition that too much investment was the cause of this first round of accelerated inflation comes from the observation that prices of investment goods increased more rapidly than other prices over these ten years.

I do not pretend to render a definitive judgment on whether the perceived constraints that initiated this response from corporate America in the early 1960s were objectively insurmountable or subjectively determined. Regarding one industry that was deeply pessimistic at the time, Jordan Lewis observes

"during the 1960s, while Zenith, G.E., and RCA treated consumer electronics as a mature business with few opportunities for significant advance, Sony, Matsushita, and JVC did the opposite . . . The Japanese foresaw consumer applications of video recording 15 years before the market could actually be tapped . . ." . . . In 1955, the U.S. output in consumer electronics was $1.5 billion, while Japanese firms produced only $70 million. Today, Japanese sales in consumer electronics are more than twice those of the United States.

It is also important to mention that the deficit financing of domestic or foreign investment did not exhaust the inflationary impact of this high-investment episode. Most American companies had adequate capacity to meet the requirement of new customers. What they needed was not so much financing for the construction of new plants, as financing for new customers to purchase the output available from existing plants. The Eurodollar market was a direct response to this need. As will be described in chapter 10, Eurodollars made an enormous contribution to the growth of world inflation.

But now I will go on to the succeeding episode of inflation. In the next chapter we will examine the more complex ways in which oil price increases added a new layer of inflation to that already created by the investment boom that has just been examined.

5

An Unnatural Disaster

There were no awaiting markets for the sticky substance that oozed out of the ground in western Pennsylvania. It was regarded as a nuisance. Initially, interest was attracted to it for its possible use as an ingredient in patent medicine, and a number of eastern interests sent a "Colonel" Drake out to see what could be done. It was Drake who conceived the idea of pumping the oil out of the ground. Once out and refined, the middle-weight distillates such as kerosene became the main lighting source in America until they were replaced later by gas and electricity.

DOUGLASS C. NORTH
Growth and Welfare in the American Past (1966)

From the end of 1973 to the end of 1981, inflation averaged 7.9 percent a year compared to 4.5 percent in the previous eight years. Unemployment rose to 6.9 percent of the labor force from 1974 through 1981 versus 4.5 percent from 1966 through 1973. Productivity stopped its growth by most measures and even reversed itself according to some. The economy went from poor to terrible. The economies of all the other major industrial countries in the world experienced similar transformations. These ubiquitous and precipitous declines in diverse aspects of well-being began in the immediate aftermath of the quadrupling of international oil prices by OPEC in late 1973 and early 1974.

It would be difficult to maintain that the oil price shocks were themselves only symptoms of economic distress rather than fundamental causes. The proximate source of the first OPEC actions was the renewed war with Israel. Close behind were a perceived reduction in the ability of the United States to enforce the interests of its corporations after the withdrawal from

38

Southeast Asia and an apparently permissive attitude on the part of the Nixon administration toward the growth of OPEC power at the expense of the seven major international oil companies. The second round of price shocks in 1979–80 also followed directly from events that were not economic but political and military: the Iranian revolution and Iran's subsequent war with Iraq.

From 1973 to 1982, international oil prices increased more than ten times—fourfold in 1973–74, another two and a half times in 1979–80, with a few extra increases in between and offsetting declines in the early 1980s. Domestic petroleum prices have now increased by a comparable amount, but the increases in coal and natural gas prices have been less. The average price of the energy products that are actually purchased by final users—gasoline, electricity, heating oil, et cetera—has increased "only" about five times. Even some portion of this increase is not a direct result of OPEC but of the continuing rise in the price of the labor and capital needed to refine, generate, and transport energy in usable forms. In 1973, about 3 percent of GNP was spent on energy. The first-round effects of a 400 percent increase in energy prices would have been only a 12 percent increase in the overall price level (3 percent of 400 percent).

In fact, the American price level doubled from 1973 to 1982. Can energy prices account for more than a small fraction of this inflation? They can, in part for reasons already given in the previous chapter. Much of the energy consumed in the American economy has the nature of a necessity. The amount purchased will not decline very much, at least for a number of years, even if the price is increased substantially. If households, businesses, or the whole country purchase even the same amount of energy at higher prices, this must necessarily take a larger fraction of total income. Other demands can be sustained at customary levels only if the prices of other things go down or if the proportion of total spending that is financed with borrowing goes up.

One could search a long time for a price that has gone down since the end of 1973. As we have already seen, it is not so easy to persuade the modern corporation to reduce its prices or to induce its work force to accept lower wages. This was the essence of Keynes's argument that we could not count on flexible prices to maintain full employment. The policies practiced since by his disciples have only increased the resistance of prices and wages to downward movements. Indeed, the initial rise in energy prices was promptly translated into increases for energy and oil-using products from Dacron to paper, fertilizers to automobiles. Increased prices led to increased wages, as workers sought to keep up with the acceleration of inflation. This, in turn, led to more increases in prices; and so round and round.

We cannot calculate with certainty how much inflation since 1973 was due to this wage-price amplification of the pure energy price effect; how much was due to the inflation already underway in the early 1970s; and how much was due to the additional effects of energy prices that will be discussed below. It is easier to analyze the consequences. Although the money price of OPEC oil increased more than ten times, general inflation cut the real price increase to about five times. For all domestically consumed energy a sixfold increase in money prices was reduced to a mere three times increase in the real quantities of labor or goods required to obtain a given amount of energy. At first, prices increased faster than wages, so that some of the cost of the OPEC increase was reflected in reduced real income for workers. In mid-1982 the real purchasing power of an hour's average wage was less than it had been in 1973. This was in sharp contrast to the increase of 2.2 percent a year in the real value of an hour's wages from the end of World War II through 1973. If the increased burdens of local taxes, federal income taxes, and Social Security taxes are taken into account, the 1982 worker had substantially less available for private consumption or saving than the worker of a decade earlier—an even sharper contrast with previous experience.

Over episodes of as long as ten years, the real wage of workers necessarily reflects changes in the real output that workers produce. Various calculations of real output per labor hour show growth roughly equal to the increase in real wages up to 1973 and close to zero change thereafter. The end of productivity growth exacerbated inflation in several ways. There is great inertia not only in the level of wages but in their rate of growth. This is because of our system of staggered expirations of three-year labor contracts. Naturally each set of business and union negotiators is inclined to match the increases established in the contracts most immediately preceding in similar industries. Annual increases granted by nonunion employers are also based on surveys of pay levels and rates of increase elsewhere. For the six years from 1968 through 1973, inclusive, wages increased by an average 6.5 percent a year within a narrow range of 6.1 percent to 7.2 percent. Productivity growth reduced these wage increases to a growth of unit labor costs and inflation of about 5 percent a year. When productivity growth disappeared, the continuing momentum of wages necessarily pulled inflation up to the 6.5 percent growth of wages plus the extra effects of the oil price increases.

But this was only the beginning. From the worker's perspective, price acceleration had suddenly eliminated the small annual gains in real purchasing power that had appeared as a matter of course for more than a quarter of a century. The solution was clearly to make wages go up enough faster to restore real gains. From 1974 through 1981, inclusive, wages increased at a new average level of over 8 percent a year, again within a narrow range of 7.2 percent to 9.0 percent. However, since more money for workers did not address the basic problem of no growth in real output per hour of work, the faster rate of gain in wages was still entirely reflected by a faster rate of gain in prices, which also increased by about 8 percent a year from 1974 through 1981. The persistent absence of real wage gains—indeed the decline in after-tax earnings and the sharp decline in discretionary earnings after taxes and such necessities as food, fuel, and mortgage payments—only increased the pressure for more rapid wage and salary increases, which in turn only increased the velocity of inflation.

The collapse of productivity improvement made an important contribution to the growth of inflation. However, the collapse itself was yet another consequence of the oil price shocks. In late 1973, the United States possessed and utilized durable capital assets with a value of about $3 trillion—more than two times that year's GNP and some thirteen times that year's very high level of expenditure for new physical assets. These capital goods—automobiles and highways, airplanes and airports, houses and stores, power plants and dishwashers, steel mills and breweries—had all been purchased, designed, and located on the assumption that, regardless of general price inflation, the relative price of oil would remain about the same. That is, these investments were designed to be worth their construction and operating expense in a world where a barrel of oil cost the same as one or two bushels of wheat, one hundredth of a ton of steel, and half an hour to an hour of an industrial worker's labor.

Since oil and energy prices have gone up considerably more than wheat, steel, or wages, these relationships have been substantially changed. A barrel of oil now trades for five or ten bushels of wheat, one fifteenth of a ton of steel, and three to five hours of an American worker's effort. What had been optimal under the old relative prices has become unavoidably inefficient under the new set of prices. An automobile designed to run 17 miles on a gallon of gasoline cannot be transformed economically into one that goes 27 miles on the same gallon. Nor can a suburban house, an hour's drive from work, be readily whisked downtown after gasoline becomes more expensive. These are just familiar examples of people being stuck with capital that can no longer be operated as it was intended to be.

Consider a salesman accustomed to using his car to visit each prospect. An increase in the price of gasoline might induce this salesman to spend less time driving and more time calling customers on the telephone. It may be that this approach results in fewer sales and commissions for the same number of hours of effort. The salesman could still sensibly choose this approach, as long as his gasoline and other travel expenses fell even more than his commission income. Productivity, measured as the volume of sales per hour of the salesman's effort, will have gone down. The salesman could have kept the statisticians happy by maintaining his productivity ratio, but only by reducing his net income.

This example is representative rather than unique. Many industrial processes require heat: brewing, distilling, extracting, refining, crystallizing, forming, forging, and drying. In most of these processes it is possible to vary the intensity of heat used and thus of energy employed. If heat intensity is reduced, one or both of two consequences usually follow in all of these processes. First, it takes longer; and/or second, a given amount of input yields less quantity or quality of final product. If both effects are present, the same machine, processing the same amount of materials, operated by the same complement of labor, takes more time to produce less output. Productivity will decline whether it is measured as the ratio of output to labor hours, output to machines, or output to some weighted combination of labor and machines.

If the price of energy goes up relative to the prices of labor, capital, and the product of their efforts, then both businesses and salesmen will be encouraged to expend more labor and capital per unit of output in order to save amounts of energy per unit of output that would have seemed quite modest under the old prices. Consider the hypothetical case of Profit Maximizing Airline Company, which owns one airplane and flies it on a single route. Under the old price regime, Profit Maximizing might schedule ten flights a day, each 60 percent full. The plane costs as much for interest and principal payments to the bank and reserves to recover the down payment, no matter how often or infrequently it is flown. Many labor costs, like the president's salary and the salaries of the staff in the airports, are also independent of the number of flights. Profit Maximizing will therefore choose to schedule frequent flights. The convenience of its schedule will attract more paying customers, while the expense of the extra flights will be relatively small (extra wages for crews and fuel costs).

When the price of fuel goes up, however, Profit Maximizing will choose to schedule fewer flights, each of which will carry more passengers. Instead of ten flights that are 60 percent full, the new schedule may have only six flights that average 80 percent full. If we measure output by the number of passengers times the number of miles flown, then output has dropped 20 percent—from 6 (60 percent of ten) to 4.8 (80 percent of 6).

However, the cost of fuel should decline in proportion to the number of flights, or by 40 percent (from ten to six). From the airline's point of view, the cost of owning the airplane does not decline because it is flown less often. The cost of labor may decline more or less than the 20 percent drop in output, depending on the division of labor between jobs that are fixed regardless of flight frequency and jobs that decline in proportion to the 40 percent drop in daily scheduled flights.

If Profit Maximizing's labor costs are half proportionate to the number of flights and half independent of flights, then they will drop by the same 20 percent as output. Output per unit of labor input, or productivity, will be unchanged. Output per unit of capital input (the one airplane) will be down by the same 20 percent as passenger-miles. However, fuel consumption will be down 40 percent, resulting in a sharp improvement in the ratio of output to use of fuel. This will always be the case for Profit Maximizing whenever the price of fuel rises relative to labor and capital. A numerical illustration of this example is provided in the notes at the end of the book.

Thus, under three quite different and representative business situations—the salesman, the industrial plant, and the airline—a rise in the relative price of energy inevitably exerts downward pressure on the productivity of both labor and capital contributions. The oil price shocks yielded inflation directly by raising certain prices, and indirectly by twirling the wage-price spiral and causing the collapse of productivity improvements. The period of falling productivity lasted for a year or two after each oil price jump, because it took a while for people to realize that relative prices had changed and that the change would last. It also took time to adjust calling schedules, operating rates, or flight schedules. Once productivity has fallen, it tends to stay at its depressed level unless and until more efficient capital at the new relative prices is put in place of old capital that has worn out or been discarded. Since automobiles rarely last much longer than ten or fifteen years and since post-1973 models are much more fuel-efficient than the 1973 fleet, most cars now in use are recent vintage, high-mileage varieties. On the other hand, the stock and, more important, the location of some capital assets changes very slowly. Such is the case with houses, subways, and bridges. In the private business sector it may take ten or twelve years before even half the value of capital represents designs and locations appropriate to the new price regime. For the economy as a whole, with dwellings and public works included in the capital stock, it will be the late 1980s before half the total reflects post-1973 prices. The location and design of the remaining half will continue to hamper efficiency. Even with new cars, trucks, and trains that minimize the use of energy, we might still have chosen to produce goods closer to their markets and to live closer to our jobs, given the new price of energy.

This process of natural replacement requires enormous patience. Even then, the only reward for enduring the pain of transition could turn out to be that the pain eventually stops, while whatever was lost remains lost forever. If the oil price increases caused us to lose 2 percent of productivity growth a year for ten years, then the loss in 1983 would amount to nearly 22 percent of GNP and a like percentage of most individual incomes, profits, dividends, and tax revenues. The total is about $750 billion, an amount almost equal to the expenditures of the federal government. If normal productivity growth resumes in 1983 or 1993, the question still remains: Will we ever recapture these enormous losses?

This could be achieved only if new technology and new capital equipment not only succeeded in offsetting the effects of higher energy costs, but also introduced a fresh leap ahead in productivity. It may be that telecommunications, microcomputers, and molecular biology are producing such extraordinary advances. However, to the extent that this is true, old capital, tied to old industries and old technologies, simply loses its value even faster. For those who own the superannuated capital or for those whose jobs depend on it, the transition becomes still more painful. For the entire economy, the increment to wealth and product exceeds the decrement to old capital and employment. But, so far, we have not reaped any bonus comparable to our loss.

The losses have been accelerated by a pace of economic obsolescence far more rapid than the rate of physical depreciation. In 1973, the bulk of business, personal, and public capital was concentrated in that complex of industries which had already experienced an exhaustion of market and technological opportunities, as explained in the previous chapter. The adverse consequences of an increase in the relative price of petroleum were particularly concentrated on those same sectors that had flourished in tandem since the early part of the century: autos and highways, electric power, appliances, suburban construction, petrochemicals, petrofertilizers, and so on. As a result, for most of the decade after 1973 the stock market valued the assets of corporate America at one half to three quarters of what it would actually cost to replace them in current condition.

This extra-rapid depreciation of the economic value of capital has three interrelated causes: the maturation and decay of the old industrial structure, the additional obsolescence caused by the increases in energy prices, and the further disadvantage imposed on traditional capital equipment by the appearance of dramatically superior techniques. Eventually the old will recede and the new triumph. We have already resumed a traditional rate of growth of output per unit of labor and capital input. It is less certain, but quite possible, that we will also experience one of those historic and infrequent bursts of advance sufficient to erase the gap that has opened since 1973 and perhaps to place us on a higher, steeper line of economic progress.

In any case, enough has been said to show why business investment since 1973 has been concentrated on new trucks and automobiles as well as on high technology equipment in computers and communications. It should also be clear why the OPEC price actions produced sharp and simultaneous increases in inflation and drops in productivity. It remains to be shown how unemployment, the third member—with inflation and productivity—of the triad of modern ills, is also an immediate consequence of the energy price increases.

The OPEC increases were peculiar in the first instance, because they affected the price of an imported product. The higher price represented additional money that went out of the United States to pay for the same volume of petroleum imports, but that money did not come back into the United States unless the OPEC countries increased their demands for American goods in proportion to the increase in their dollar revenues. For the most part, this did not happen. Consequently, the price increase had the same effect as would have obtained if the federal government had imposed an additional excise tax on gasoline and heating oil, using the proceeds to reduce its borrowing or to retire debt. As we have seen, unless money taken from one part of the economy is returned to another, there will be a commensurate decline in effective demand and employment.

In order to neutralize the unemployment effect of the OPEC tax, the federal government should have increased its own expenditures as if it were the recipient of the new OPEC revenues. The required increase in the federal deficit for the eight years from 1974 through 1981 was about $45 billion a year, or over 2 percent of GNP. In fact, the increase in the average deficit from the eight years ending 1973 to the following eight years, was only 0.9 percent of GNP. The inflationary consequences of OPEC, on top of the serious inflation already under way in 1973, turned both monetary policy and fiscal policy (government taxing and spending) toward fighting inflation instead of unemployment.

In 1973, inflation was already well-established at 5 percent, with every indication that our economic structure would keep it there or cause it to accelerate further. The argument at the beginning of this chapter suggests that the direct effects of the oil price shocks would have added another 12 percent to prices over the first eight years plus 2 percent a year because of the disappearance of productivity improvements. Thus, the rate of inflation should have increased by about 3.5 percent a year plus any spontaneous acceleration that might have been generated by this leap. In fact, anti-inflationary policy succeeded in holding the increase in inflation to about two thirds of a percentage point below this number. From 1974 through 1981, inflation averaged 7.85 percent compared to 5 percent in the previous six years, an increase of only 2.85 percent.

On the one hand, this policy was viewed as a failure since inflation had actually increased considerably, albeit less than it

might have. On the other hand, the price paid for keeping inflation 0.65 percent a year lower than it would have been was an
increase of 1.5 percent in the average annual rate of unemployment, on top of a rate that had already seemed alarming before
OPEC. The anguish experienced by economic policymakers in
the 1950s and 1960s was undiminished in the 1970s, although
the policies were reversed. In the first instance, reductions in
unemployment had led to inflation that was unexpectedly large
and early. Then a substantial, prolonged, and deliberately induced rise in unemployment produced disappointingly slight
reductions in inflation.

In part this policy "tradeoff" appeared particularly unattractive because the oil price increases had specific employment-
depressing influences beside the dollar drain on effective demand. Under the old relative prices, Profit Maximizing Airlines
flew its plane 60 percent full, ten times a day. Imagine that this
was the greatest possible number of daily flights. In that case,
increases in demand for air travel would have led promptly to
increases in the investment demand for aircraft. However,
under the new price regime, Profit Maximizing flies its plane
only six times a day, 80 percent full. The price of tickets has
gone up faster than other prices because of the heavy fuel use in
air travel. The convenience of schedules has decreased. For
both reasons demand has fallen from six full plane loads a day
to 4.8. Profit Maximizing's optimal capacity, however, is still
ten flights a day, each 80 percent full, or a total of eight full
plane loads. Demand can increase from 4.8 to 8, or by two
thirds, without generating any new orders for aircraft. The
salesman's use of his car is a similar story. Employment in the
aircraft and automobile industries is devastated, in addition to
the 20 percent drop in Profit Maximizing's work force. And all
of this is in addition to the overall demand-reducing effects of
the OPEC surplus.

The energy-intensive industries, producing products that are
often also intensive energy users, were already facing saturated
demand and declining efficiency and profitability. Recent investment by these industries had already been financed by substantial borrowing of questionable viability. The increased rela-

tive price of energy fired a lethal torpedo into an already foundering ship. After 1973, investment in aircraft and railroads, almost all categories of industrial machinery, farm machinery, construction machinery, engines, and electric utility equipment has been declining in real volume, although other categories of investment have continued to grow. The impact on total demand and employment was substantial, because these impacted categories accounted for 45 percent of all business investment in 1970. By 1980, these groups had declined to 32 percent of business investment, and the negative effect of their decline on total employment was correspondingly lessened.

A government whose Keynesian commitment to full employment had not been daunted would have responded to these declines in investment by increasing its expenditure or encouraging more loan expenditures to offset these declines in business investment as well as the funds extracted and not respent by OPEC. In actuality, deficit spending did not cover even the latter shortfall, let alone the former. Monetary policy strove consistently to make private borrowing and spending more difficult by raising interest rates even faster than inflation.

A few points need to be made more explicit to avoid any misunderstanding. Although the increase in the average federal deficit, from 1.25 percent of GNP in the eight years through 1973 to 2.15 percent in the eight years thereafter, was insufficient to offset the direct and indirect depressing effects of OPEC, it does not necessarily follow that the relative increases in the deficits under President Reagan are a proper remedy for past errors. The Reagan deficits will add an additional 3 percent to 4 percent of GNP to the previous base. Since oil imports and relative oil prices are now declining, while the investment impact on energy-intensive industries is also declining, these deficits could easily be too large compared to the actual need in the early 1980s. (For more on the Reagan deficits, see chapter 17.)

The second point has to do with prices. It is a fundamental principle of conventional economics that prices in a capitalist system—even a very imperfect capitalist system—contain enormous amounts of valid information. Indeed, it is held to be almost beyond organized human effort to perceive as much as is writ large by the Invisible Hand in the form of prices produced by the conjunction of market supply with market demand. It is easy to show undergraduates and newspaper readers that, if a misguided city government should interfere with the market by imposing rent control, then land, labor, and capital previously employed in the construction of apartments will be diverted to more remunerative activities. The last unit built, if any are, will continue to entail the cost just covered by the controlled rent. Thus many would-be tenants will find their demands unsatisfied, although the last tenants housed will be especially pleased with their bargains.

It is clear that the users of energy also adjust their consumption to reflect cost as the relative price changes. However, it is also clear that enormous existing stocks of capital dictate limits on the intensity of energy used to operate the economy and that these intensities can be changed significantly only over long periods of time. It should be equally clear, although I have not belabored the point, that the price of oil, both before and after 1973, was determined by the monopoly power of its sellers rather than by some rational calculation of the economic and social costs of its production.

Before 1973, it cost about 10¢ a barrel to produce oil in Saudi Arabia. Today's cost may be 30¢ a barrel. The effective cost of oil from the North Sea or Alaska's North Slope is close to $25 a barrel. The social cost of exhausting this finite natural resource depends on our estimates of the amounts yet to be exploited, the prospects for replacement technologies, and the value assigned to the needs of future generations and to the needs of countries that have not yet industrialized. Did $2 a barrel in 1973 equate demand and supply at a price that reflected the market's full wisdom on these topics? Did $25 a barrel a few years later? Or $40 a few years after that?

Two considerations shed some light on this question. Most of the petroleum and natural gas produced in the world today was already being willingly and profitably produced at pre-1973 prices from the same fields by the same producers. Most of today's consumption is determined by capital structures that were also in place before 1973. For these reasons, the energy policy that was finally adopted by the United States in 1980 was basically sound. The price of oil to consumers has been moved rapidly toward the prevailing world price. The increase in natural gas prices has been subjected to a more gradual and controlled increase, since enormous additional domestic supplies are available and many significant capital commitments by consumers and businesses were based on past prices. The increased revenues to producers of old oil has been subjected to a windfall profits tax, which is available in principle to aid disadvantaged consumers. The current high world price has been made fully available to those who discover and produce new oil.

This is certainly a superior policy to the paralysis that prevailed for the first seven years after the initial price shock. However, there is considerable reason to doubt whether the supply response induced by recent high prices is economically rational. At recent prices for fish and oil it is not hard to demonstrate that it would "pay" to destroy marine life and the annual fish catch on Georges Bank forever in return for the discovery and exploitation of a 3- to 5-billion-barrel oil reserve. But anyone with sufficient innocence of economics surely would question the wisdom of destroying one of the world's prolific sources of edible fish for all eternity in return for as much oil as the United States consumes in six to ten months.

6

The Inertia
of Inflation

Something has to be different now. The difference in
what exists today must stem from what has happened
in the past. The intensity of inflation that is maintained
in a weak economy simply must reflect the inflationary
history that preceded it. Some insidious ratchet has
gone into operation, giving inflation a far greater degree of persistence than it ever had before. But who
threw the ratchet into the soup?

ARTHUR OKUN
Prices and Quantities (1980)

Thus far I have had frequent occasion to make passing reference to the ways in which inflation is self-perpetuating or even
self-accelerating. It is now time to look at those mechanisms in
more detail. Their importance by the early 1980s derived from
the fact that the higher the rate of inflation and the longer the
experience of inflation, the more inflation itself becomes the
principal explanation of inflation.

Our economy is replete with arrangements to make the
money prices of things less flexible and more predictable. No
one starts each workday by renegotiating that day's pay with an
employer. We would not find this to be a convenient or productive arrangement, even though each day might bring changes in
the strength of the employer's business or in the number of
applicants for a job at some higher or lower rate of pay. It
would no longer be rational to examine alternative television
sets or necklaces in a number of different stores before deciding
on a purchase, if shoppers could not believe that the price tags
on these goods were going to remain the same from one hour or

day to the next. It has long been customary for tenants (residential or business) to agree with their landlords on a fixed rent for anywhere from one to twenty years. Home buyers and their banks reach similar agreement on a long stream of fixed mortgage payments. Indeed, almost all borrowing and lending represents, by definition, a contract for which the money payments are fixed in advance.

The advantage of these arrangements is that they enable people to plan for the near and distant future without the awesome uncertainty that would otherwise exist. They also eliminate enormous effort that would otherwise be devoted to continuously determining and resetting prices. They encourage lasting and specialized relationships between the exchanging parties. Workers can obtain and employers impart the skills of peculiar value in a particular industry or workplace. Tenants are encouraged to improve their leaseholds. Businesses can compute the "standard cost" of their products, based on posted prices and known rates for labor and rent. A conventional markup applied to standard cost provides some assurance of profits.

The knowledge buyers and sellers have about prices for comparable goods and services is the immediate determinant of most fixed prices. Both employers and workers make it their business to know something about the prevailing levels of pay at other establishments. Retailers check their competitors' prices, as do their customers. Everyone desires to maintain relative position in terms of money by doing exactly what everyone else does. This imparts great inertia to the structure of wages and prices and to any static level of prices or established rate of change of prices. Nobody wants to be the first to break an established pattern. The duration for which prices are fixed is established by custom and contract in various markets. The desire of everyone to imitate everyone else is best accommodated when the renewal dates of long contracts are spread evenly over time rather than bunched together. This is obviously the case with bank lending, and it is true as well for the timing of expirations of three-year contracts between employers and unions.

There is nothing about a world of fixed prices that implies

necessary inflation. On the contrary, because its prices and wages respond slowly and reluctantly to pressures up or down, such a world is quite compatible with a stable price level. Even if average prices were stable, individual price series would still fluctuate over time or show persistent trends one way or the other. Some products, like those of agriculture, continue to trade in flexible price markets, resembling those in classical textbooks. Although government price supports prevent it from falling too far, the price of wheat is not fixed; it varies by the minute in grain pits and futures markets that are organized like the stock exchanges. Prices react swiftly to fluctuations in the weather or in export demand.

In the fixed-price sector some prices must necessarily increase over time while others decline, even though price changes are small and infrequent compared to those in the wheat market. This is so because wages and other costs will be the same for different businesses, while changes in productivity will differ. Employers hiring workers with comparable skills and experience to do comparable work in the same location must pay roughly comparable wages—just as they pay the same rent for buildings or price for electricity—regardless of how productively they can employ what they have hired. Firms that enjoy steady increases in productivity will experience falling standard costs at any given level of wages and other input prices. Such firms will be impelled either to lower prices in step with costs or to maintain prices and raise wages in step with productivity growth.

The largest corporations in major capitalist countries followed the latter course by explicitly agreeing with their unions to increase wages at the apparent average rate of increase in labor productivity. The prototype in the United States was the "General Motors Formula," agreed to by the company and the United Auto Workers in 1948 after three years of postwar labor-management struggle. The General Motors agreement also established the precedent of anticipating productivity improvements over the subsequent three years, which became the standard length of union contracts.

These improvement factors in wage increases averaged the

same 2 percent to 3 percent a year that labor productivity was improving in all American manufacturing. Industries whose productivity performance was superior to this benchmark were thereby enabled to exercise price restraint, while the products of industries with below-average productivity performance were subject to upward price pressure.

There were two inflationary consequences of this seemingly innocent arrangement. One was immediate; the other, delayed. The productivity improvements experienced by large manufacturing corporations were generally superior to those experienced by many smaller firms and personal businesses providing labor-intensive services (such as beauty parlors, hotels, and insurance agents). Moreover, the most rapidly growing component of employment was the public sector, especially for services at the local level, where productivity increases were even more minimal. The manufacturing sector set a pay standard with which other employers were obliged to compete. As wages rose faster than productivity in these sectors, prices (or taxes and deficits) necessarily rose. The economy therefore experienced some inflation even when products of the rapidly improving manufacturing sector showed no average increase.

Inflation in the cost of restaurant meals and lawyers meant increased costs for the major corporations and their workers. The principle of protecting the workers was already incorporated in the General Motors Formula through the innovative introduction of a cost-of-living adjustment (or COLA), which automatically augmented workers' wages by a function of the actual increase in the Consumer Price Index during the life of the contract, on top of the predetermined productivity improvement increases. This in turn raised the rate of wage increase that had to be matched by the lagging sectors. It also affected the major corporations, who passed these increases in labor costs, along with the increases in public and private service costs, on to the consumer in the form of higher prices. Thus, each cost and price increase tended to reverberate in additional increases elsewhere.

In the 1950s and early 1960s the fixed-price system got sorted out into a system that anticipated a fixed rate of increase in the average price level. Hourly wages in the manufacturing sector increased by 2 percent a year for productivity plus another 2 percent for inflation. Wages elsewhere increased by the same 4 percent. Lenders and borrowers who had been happy with 2.5 percent interest rates in 1955 were equally satisfied with 4.5 percent in 1965. Many long-term rents and contracts to deliver commodities also embodied the anticipated rate of inflation. The inclusion of these expectations in contracts tended to make them self-fulfilling. If wages, rents, interest rates, and pricing strategies anticipated 2 percent inflation, there was little realistic prospect that actual inflation would be less than 2 percent, although there remained a significant potential that it would be greater.

The second inflationary consequence emerged as soon as the secular rate of productivity improvement began to decline. The improvement factor was an anticipation of the average rate of productivity advance among the major corporations. As I have argued in chapter 4, an increasing number of industries encountered disappointing productivity trends, starting in the early 1960s. The possibility of temporary reversals and cyclical aberrations in productivity advance had been recognized from the onset. Accordingly, the improvement factor remained fixed, indeed somewhat elevated, around 3 percent at just the time that it was losing justification. Indeed for most workers, whether or not they were represented by unions, a 2 percent a year improvement in real wages had come to seem more like an entitlement than a bonus contingent upon the remote outcome of macroeconomic events. In the same way, nonunionized and many unionized workers took their inflation adjustment in the form of an additional fixed increase of roughly 2 percent a year rather than a formula cost-of-living adjustment.

As one leading industry after another encountered saturated markets or diminishing economies of scale, the fixed improvement factor became increasingly a net increment to inflation. The acceleration of inflation only intensified the determination of workers to obtain wage increases that continued to exceed inflation by 2 percent a year. It is therefore not surprising that actual and effectively anticipated inflation increased from 2 percent before 1965 to about 5 percent from the late 1960s to the early 1970s. As suggested in chapter 3, some portion of this acceleration was due to the prolonged and successful war on unemployment that was waged by the Kennedy and Johnson administrations. A lesser portion was due to the ill-conceived and ill-financed shooting war in Southeast Asia, pursued by the same administrations.

We saw in the last chapter that the OPEC price increase of 1973 and the subsequent increases in the late 1970s had the effect of totally eliminating productivity growth for the entire economy. The result was to translate all of the accustomed increase in nominal wages and salaries into a perfectly proportionate increase in prices. After 1973, wages, interest rates, and prices adjusted to still higher rates of anticipated inflation. Indeed, there is nothing in our system that prevents the anticipation of a constant rate of acceleration of inflation. As the 1970s unfolded, such anticipations of a constant rate of increase in the rate of increase of prices became the standard that was embodied in contracts.

By now it should be clear that inflation extends itself by causing people to expect more of it. The longer and higher our experience of inflation has already been the more certainly do we expect inflation to persist longer and higher into the future. In our economy these expectations are incorporated into the interest rates that lenders require and borrowers are willing to pay, the wages that workers demand and employers think they can afford, the long-term contracts under which mines sell coal to electric utilities, and a great number of similar arrangements. In every case, the expectation of inflation today contributes to inflationary increases in contractual costs for many tomorrows.

The homeowner who agrees to pay 17 percent mortgage interest must seek the expected inflationary increases in his or her compensation in order to make ends meet. The business that commits itself to pay high interest and increasing wages must charge higher prices in order to cover its costs. The coal mine, hospital, or weapons manufacturer with a contractual guarantee from the customer to pay for cost increases will obviously have no motive to resist higher costs when they emerge.

It is for these reasons that people speak knowingly of an "embedded" rate of inflation in the economy. Consider a typical large American corporation at the midpoint of a three-year contract with its unions. Of the revenues that it retains after purchases from other corporations, about 8 percent are pre-tax profits (give or take 1 percent, depending on whether or not one corrects reported profits for the distortions of inflation). By contrast, about 67 percent is used to pay compensation, fringe benefits, and payroll taxes for employees. Under a typical contract, these costs are scheduled to increase about 6 percent a year before any additional adjustments for actual inflation—2 percent to 3 percent for a traditional improvement factor and 3 percent to 4 percent for the portion of anticipated inflation that is not covered by cost-of-living adjustments. The remaining costs—interest, depreciation, and property and excise taxes— are largely fixed.

Now suppose, merely for the sake of illustration, that price inflation is brought to an immediate halt. As will be apparent in a moment, it would be very optimistic under such circumstances to assume that the level of production and productivity would be maintained. With zero inflation, the corporation's revenues would be constant. However, over the remaining year and a half of its labor contract, labor costs would rise by 9 percent (6 percent for a year and a half), or from 67 percent of total income to 73 percent (109 percent of 67 percent). As a result, over the same year and a half, profits would necessarily drop from about 8 percent to about 2 percent, or by 75 percent. A plunge of this magnitude for the average corporation would clearly leave many corporations in even worse circumstances—for example, those whose profit margins were lower than average to begin with or those who had just signed new three-year contracts. Even those firms whose contracts expired immediately after inflation's demise might have trouble believing that it was really dead and convincing the autoworkers or steelworkers to accept no increase when the coal miners were still enjoying large increases won previously.

Profit-making businesses would not passively accept this destruction. They would try first to protect their profits by raising prices sufficiently to cover increasing costs. If they succeeded, the hypothesized end of inflation would be illusory. If they failed, they would still attempt to protect profits by firing expensive employees and reducing unprofitable production. These cutbacks would further reduce demand for the products of other businesses that were already weakened by disinflation. Falling production, employment, incomes, and demand would cumulate to disastrous proportions.

We can now answer Arthur Okun's question with which this chapter began: Who threw the ratchet into the soup so that inflation tends to persist? The answer is no one and everyone. The essence of the soup is the ratchet. The soup is the way we have learned to conduct most of our economic affairs so that the level of prices or the rate of change of prices can be incorporated into our myriad plans with some assurance. It is a system especially suited to the reality that most contemporary goods and services are the results of long periods of prior preparation and exhibit manifold variety as to quality, style, color, location, atmosphere, or personality. A reality, in short, that is quite different from the world of homogeneous bushels of wheat and malleable factory hands on which the classical economic model is based.

None of this constitutes a recently arrived state of affairs. The skills and products of labor have been complexly and finely diverse since before the Industrial Revolution. The large corporation looms no larger in our economy today than it did at the beginning of this century. Wages and prices that are persistent, posted, published, or tagged have always characterized industrial economies. The enlarged role of labor unions is a new factor. Three-year collective bargaining agreements have certainly added some persistence to the level and rate of change of prices and wages. However, 80 percent of the American labor force does not belong to a union. For these workers, periodic adjustments of pay still reflect longer-term expectations held implicitly by the employer and employee and the continuous stampede of everyone catching up with everyone else.

The inertia of the rate of change of prices is only a small generalization from the inertia of the level of prices upon which

Keynes's explanation of unemployment rests. Both derive from the same inflexibility of prices and labor incomes in response to short-run fluctuations in demand. The decisive proof of all this is that inflations have exhibited persistence and a tendency to accelerate for all of recorded history. As we shall see in Part III, a graph of the rate of inflation over the past few centuries looks like the teeth of a saw: Each epoch of increasing prices begins slowly and accelerates to a peak from which prices drop vertically to set the stage for the next episode. In 1923, Keynes made a commonplace observation: "It is characteristic of the impetuosity of the credit cycle that price movements tend to be cumulative, each movement promoting, up to a certain point, a further movement in the same direction."

In the next chapter and those following it, I shall look more closely at the determinants of the "certain point" at which inflation stops and the vertical decline in the sawtooth pattern commences. First, it is important to pause for a recapitulation. An answer has now been developed to the basic question with which I have been concerned from the beginning of this book. The stubborn coexistence of inflation and unemployment results from the interaction of price inflexibility, Keynesian policies, and a confluence of aging industries and OPEC.

In addition to the historical and political reasons for the Keynesian state to exert more effort to contain unemployment than to contain inflation, we have revealed a very rational foundation for such a bias. In a world of fixed costs and prices, if inflation is attacked by the conventional Keynesian weapons—higher taxes, less government spending, or higher interest rates—almost all of the initial effect of reduced borrowing and spending will be in the form of reduced production and employment rather than in lower inflation. Indeed, if restrictive measures are applied when the system is still adjusting to a higher level of inflation, the rate of price increase may actually accelerate at the same time that unemployment is also increasing.

Employing such methods, governments would have to administer large and prolonged doses of unemployment to produce comparatively modest progress against inflation. But as we have seen, unemployment also generates more unemployment, while eventual success at disinflation only compounds the unemployment problem. Arthur Okun, who had major responsibility for resolving this dilemma in the United States in the 1960s, concluded that

> when demand management is conducted with a reasonable degree of sophistication, policymakers do not, and should not, accept secular deflation . . . [If] the inflation strategy relies solely on demand restraint, it is likely to impose large social costs from recession and prolonged slack . . . [It] may be less costly to accept the higher secular inflation rate on a permanent basis than to pursue a strategy to roll it back.

Private prices and pay arrangements quickly adjust to the perception that each new level of inflation becomes an effective minimum for reasons of state as well as inertia. Since only increases in inflation are permissible, it is only a matter of time until they occur. It is in this context that we can fully appreciate the effects of the intensified assault on unemployment during the 1960s, the simultaneous productivity problems in many important industries, and the OPEC price shocks of the 1970s.

It is fair to say that the near 7 percent unemployment from 1974 through 1979 and the substantially higher and rising levels thus far in the 1980s are the high price that the federal government has chosen to pay to keep the rate of inflation about 1 percent a year lower than it would otherwise have been in the 1970s, and to lower it perhaps a bit more in the early years of this decade.

7

How Inflations Die

Of all that was done in the past, you eat the fruit, either
rotten or ripe.

T. S. ELIOT
"Choruses from 'The Rock' " (1934)

We have spent some time examining the roots of inflation. Indeed, I have looked at a good part of its trunk and branches. I will now consider the fruits.

Over time, our economy incorporates inflation into contracts and behavior patterns. The rate of inflation implicit in these arrangements has been called, variously, the accustomed, adopted, or anticipated rate of inflation. The economist George Perry has dubbed it the "habitual" rate of inflation. The latter term has the advantage of conveying a sense of the dependence that we develop for the inflation to which we adapt. To emphasize this aspect, I shall refer to the addictive rate of inflation. The relation of the economy to inflation is much the same as that between an addict and heroin. We need continuing injections. Withdrawing cold turkey could be fatal. At the same time, our habit does us no good and much harm.

The addictive nature of inflation is only a different perspective on the persistence described in the previous chapter. Employers who are committed, explicitly or implicitly, to continuing increases in wages and other costs, must necessarily receive the higher prices on which those commitments were based; or profits, production, and employment will collapse. The family that buys a house it could not afford by conventional, pre-inflation standards and finances it with a large mortgage at 17 percent must experience continuing inflation in its income, the price of the house, or both, to avoid the risk of insolvency.

62

One of the ways that businesses and households accommo-date or addict themselves to inflation is by increasing their debt even as interest rates on that debt anticipate higher rates of inflation. In a period of rising prices, everyone wants to buy now and pay later. This general stimulus to universal deficit spending is one of the important avenues through which antici-pated inflation becomes realized inflation. The debt obligations that remain are an important reason why both become addic-tive inflation. Corporations that lose their profits, cut their production, and lay off their workers are also likely to default on their debts. Workers who lose their jobs will default on their mortgages and auto loans. A local government containing too many of such businesses and workers in its domain may well have to default on its debts as well.

A sudden advent of price stability implies an avalanche of bankruptcies. One failing business or debtor knocks down oth-ers. Creditors suffer lost wealth or income. Closed businesses and unemployed workers mean reduced demand for the prod-ucts of other businesses and workers, leading to more closings and layoffs. After banks foreclosed on their collateral, there would be a glut of factories and houses offered for sale in a dead market. For all of these reasons, price stability would become downward *in*stability. Falling prices would create problems for still more businesses and for other debtors with inflated wages, interest, rents, or taxes to pay. In short, a precipitous end to inflation invites a deadly whirlpool of deflation and depression. The higher the rate of inflation to which we are addicted, the more fatal a sudden withdrawal is likely to be.

Any national government or central bank that is aware of this danger is likely to continue administering sufficient monetary and fiscal stimulus to keep inflation from disappearing. Even private banks find themselves increasingly in the position of lending their customers new money for the purpose of paying principal and interest on previous loans. Except for an occa-sional high drama, involving debtors like Mexico, this indul-gence of lenders toward debtors has nothing to do with fear of the social consequences for the entire economy. Banks are al-ways reluctant to put loans in default and foreclose on collateral for reasons of practicality and expense. They are always anxious to continue accommodating existing customers out of regard for long-term growth and profitability. The enlarged fraction of credit that simply refinances previous credit reflects the plain arithmetic of inflation. A larger fraction of "growth" for all economic units is in the form of price increases and a declining fraction in the form of real additions to output, employment, capital, or inventories.

In addition to the momentum of habitual inflation and the addictive quality of the associated debt, inflation also encourages the growth of hidden debts, which become equally effective spurs to renewed inflation. The primary example is the growth of pension promises in excess of the resources set aside to fund them. On the one hand, rising inflation caused workers in the public and the private sector to demand increased wages and benefits. In addition, current recipients of Social Security and some private pension benefits sought cost-of-living adjustments. On the other hand, the natural myopic tendencies of businessmen and politicians were reinforced by the expectation of continuing or increasing inflation. If it made sense to sell dept that was a promise to pay in the future in exchange for cash that could be spent today, then it made equal sense to make pension promises for the future in exchange for cooperative workers and quiescent beneficiaries today.

The results of this natural squeeze have been surprisingly large. For many states and cities, which came under severe wage and inflation catch-up pressure in the past twenty years, unfunded pension liabilities now have a value equivalent to all outstanding debt. The relative burden is not quite so large for private corporations. Even so, some large companies have future pension promises still to be paid for, worth more than their total equity. But the pioneer and champion issuer of future pension promises is the federal government. The payments that the federal government has promised to its own workers and Social Security recipients, already in the work force or retired, will require about six times as much money as all future payments of principal and interest on the national debt. Or, put differently, promised Social Security and government pensions will require more money than the future service of all the outstanding debt of all American nonfinancial businesses, individuals, families, units of local government, and the federal government combined.

These hidden debts must be paid, no less than visible ones. Steel companies must raise their prices to pay pensions as well as wages. States and municipalities are obliged to raise taxes for labor services obtained in the past as well as the present. The federal government has maintained the fiction that Social Security is an insurance program rather than a transfer of income from those presently paying taxes to those presently retired. This fiction has been used to cover a massive shift of the federal tax burden away from those most able to pay and in a pro-inflation direction long before the Reagan administration began its crusade to rescue the rich.

While the federal income tax is intended to be progressive and fair by exempting low levels of income, permitting deductions, and taxing higher amounts of income at higher rates, the Social Security tax accomplishes the exact opposite. Income from dividends, interest, rents, and capital gains is excluded from the tax along with winnings at the race track. Only income from work is subject to the tax. Even then, all earned income *over* $35,700 (in 1983) is exempted. Of what remains, the first dollar is taxed at the same rate as the last. It would be difficult to devise a scheme more devilishly efficient at throwing a maximum share of the burden onto the lowest-income workers, discouraging work altogether and needlessly promoting inflation. The latter effect results from the portion of the tax that is paid directly by employers. This payroll tax increases labor costs— and consequently prices—without any demand having been made for, or increase granted in, the actual pay of workers.

There was a time when many pension obligations could be eased by continuing inflation in the same way as debt obligations. A promise to pay any fixed amount of dollars always becomes less expensive as inflation makes the dollars less valuable. However, as pensions, and especially Social Security, have been indexed and over-indexed to inflation, inflation no longer reduces the burden. Nevertheless, the costs of paying the pensions remains a cause of more inflation.

If excessive promises cannot be inflated away, they must be

broken. That is the essence of the vertical drops that have terminated previous prolonged periods of inflation in panics of debt default and depression. Before this book is printed, the federal government may take the lead by modestly reducing its always pliable promises to make Social Security payments. The real question, to which I shall return at the end, is whether we can devise a prolonged series of small steps that will enable us to back out of inflation as slowly and harmlessly as we wandered into it. From New York City to Chrysler and Poland, the fear of default and collapse has brought public policy to the side of refinance and reinflation.

There are good habits as well as bad. If breaking our addiction to inflation entails such risk of harm and requires such exertion of imagination, we had best be certain that escaping our dependence is worth these dangers and efforts. Who loses what from continuing inflation? It is tautological that the immediate losers are the holders of money, in proportion to the amounts they hold, since inflation is a decrease in the value of those holdings. The definition of this group of losers should be slightly expanded to include the ownership of assets that are good substitutes for money and the possession of superior access to money. Thus, the owners of stocks and bonds, banks, and other lenders are all prominent among the relative losers from inflation. Their losses may be ameliorated to the extent that interest rates on deposits and loans, or the returns on common stocks, keep pace with inflation.

By this simple reasoning, the winners from inflation would be the negative of the losers: the penniless instead of the monied, borrowers instead of lenders, owners of real assets instead of money assets. When I took American history in high school, this was the essential picture that was painted of the followers of William Jennings Bryan, arrayed against the urban plutocrats whose champion was McKinley. It seemed to follow that the proponents of more wealth more justly distributed would be advocates of inflation, while the defenders of established wealth, mal-distributed, would attempt to nail prices and progress to a cross of gold.

Consistent with this view there is a rough historical correlation between high employment, high growth, more uniform distribution of income, and more inflation. As is so often the case, it is not so clear which of these may be causes of the others, or whether all are symptoms of additional forces. We have already seen that the Keynesian advocates of employment, growth, and equity set off, knowingly and otherwise, in an inflationary direction. On the other hand, the inflation instigated by OPEC was a simultaneous enemy of economic advance and jobs.

So, we have uncovered only a Byzantine reason for seeking a painless exit from inflation. Like anything else that attacks established wealth, inflation is likely to provoke a counter assault from the wealthy. For reasons that may sometimes have at least a historical justification, the assault is likely to be against arrangements that promote economic security, productivity, and jobs. This makes it all the more likely that inflation will end in a disastrous tumult.

Therefore, in addition to generating self-sustaining momentum, inflations are the social catalysts for their own destruction. As we have seen, it is also possible that inflations contain self-destructing mechanisms of an economic nature. It is certain that the more long-standing the addiction to and the higher the dose of inflation, the more vulnerable the economy is to collapse in the face of an even modest cessation of inflation. If such lapses in the administration of price increases can be caused by random accidents—good crops, productive new technologies, the collapse of OPEC, a sudden epidemic of peace—then the likelihood of collapse increases with the mere passage of time and increase of vulnerability.

Perhaps inflations even contribute to their own terminations in more systematic ways. For example, every inflation of which we have knowledge has continuously undermined the nominal value of all financial assets, with real values falling proportionately more. To the extent that individuals hold more wealth in financial assets than in real assets (that may keep up with inflation), this implies a deterioration in real wealth at any constant rate of saving. If inflation encourages more consumption and borrowing at the expense of saving, wealth will decline even more rapidly. All of this seems to have happened in recent decades, while the value of financial assets remained above or near half that of all personal assets. Meanwhile, debt increases, not only in proportion to inflation but faster than incomes and wealth. Thus individuals find the burden of debt growing relative to income and assets, while the value of assets shrinks relative to what seems adequate for present and future security. Eventually these forces must drive the savings rate up (in order to reduce relative debt and increase wealth), thus reversing the downward drift of savings that is caused by and perpetuates more of inflation.

All of these matters are better understood than they are discussed in public, as was true of sex until recent times. As inflations persist and accelerate, the tensions between self-sustaining and self-destroying impulses grow more intense. That is why inflations become more volatile and unpredictable as they age and accelerate. In particular, the growing risk of reversal explains why interest rates usually do not fully reflect a future inflation as high as in the immediate past. This was true of our recent inflation until the Federal Reserve chose to drive interest rates higher after October 1979. The disastrous consequences of a reversal also prevent stock prices from valuing inflated earnings and dividends as generously as the results of real growth.

Thus our choice is to end our addiction in a deliberate way, planned to minimize the damage, or to have it ended for us in a haphazard and destructive fashion. To the extent that inflation destroys money, its continuance may be as damaging as its cessation, and this gives us a more common basis for joining against inflation. For as we shall see in the next Part, money is a vital essence of our collective existence.

PART II

Hats, Rabbits, and Money

8

The Veil
of Materialism

You cannot ride on a claim to a horse, but you can pay
with a claim to money.

JOSEPH A. SCHUMPETER
History of Economic Analysis (1954)

More often than not, economists have believed that money
serves to conceal the "real" economic activity of persons at
work, bushels of wheat harvested, tons of steel produced, or
automobiles scrapped. Economists are perhaps more inclined
than most professionals to fortify their argot with expressions
like *The Veil of Money*. The idea that money had nothing important to do with the real questions of economics was so outra-
geously dumbfounding that it admirably performed the role of
separating the holy priesthood from the ignorant masses and
initiating neophytes by their ceremonial ingestion of such
unappealing mouthfuls. For the lay observer or participant, the
veil appears quite significant. Money and such closely related
abstractions as stocks, bonds, and mortgages are the very things
that we are frenetically engaged in acquiring, dispensing, re-
deeming, and accumulating. In the absence of these insubstan-
tial symbols, our society would become a beehive without
honey.

Since we cannot eat our bonds or money as the bees eat their
honey, it is clearly the case that we must be doing something
else with it to obtain the necessities and luxuries of life. While
we perceive ourselves as acquiring and exchanging money and
its related paraphernalia, many of us are in fact provisioning
society with food, clothing, shelter, nuclear submarines, and

71

books. In this sense, money is not so much a veil as an organizing principle of our productive activity. The metaphoric aphorism of economists should be reformulated perhaps to cast us in the role of dumb horses, unknowingly powering a treadmill in the endless pursuit of the carrot, money.

This is still not a very helpful image. In contrast to the presumed ignorance of the horses, most of us are quite aware of the treadmill and conscious of the fact that we are canning tomatoes, driving a bus, writing a book, or whatever else it is that we do for a living. In further contrast, our treadmill drives machines that produce an opulent splendor of things, most of which go to the horses rather than to some master. Finally, horses eat carrots, but we still cannot eat money.

If this inedible stuff really is an important part of how our system works, it must achieve its effects (alone or in concert with other factors) in oblique ways.

Invariably, when economists or philosophers set out to explain the nature and functions of money, they do so by means of a historical narrative. The sequence that is adduced depends even more than most history on the logic of the situation rather than on our knowledge of it.

In the beginning, a unit of human economic activity must have been a family or a tribe or a herd, much as is the case with other, undomesticated mammals. Whatever the unit, it must have been economically self-contained, in the sense that it consumed whatever it obtained and obtained whatever it consumed. Nothing was obtained by one unit for the purpose of exchanging it for the possessions of another. Nor, therefore, was anything obtained by exchange. This also is true of wild animals, whether they forage or hunt.

The first great event in this epic is the emergence of trading. Logic and evidence suggest that humans began to swap one kind of property for another in very ancient times, perhaps as long ago as the origin of language. The earliest Stone Age hunters made tools, clothed themselves with the furs and skins of animals, and fed themselves with both the fauna and the flora of their natural environments. Trading among different economic units would be natural and beneficial to the extent that they occupied regions with differing endowments of flint and obsidian, berries and nuts, animals that were furry or succulent. An even greater stimulus to trade might have been provoked by differences among communities in the proficiency with which various practical arts were performed.

The frequency and complexity of those exchanges presumably increased with the expansion of domesticated crops and animals and the attendant proliferation of civilized occupations and products. These tens of thousands of years, during which people exchanged goods only by means of barter, are distinguished in the history of money not by any fixity of culture, economy, or technology but instead by the mere fact that these exchanges were accomplished without the use of money.

Pure logic demonstrates that the specialization of tasks and diversity of products made possible by barter were a great improvement over self-sufficiency. It is equally a matter of logic that money must have multiplied the potential complexity, divisibility, and timing of transactions in ways that enabled us to elevate our material existence still farther above the original subsistence.

The first problem that money solves is this. If I have a pig and wish to use it to acquire a knife and a tunic, under a system of barter it may well be that a pig exchanges for two knives or for three tunics. In that case, a knife would be worth one and a half tunics. I could swap my pig for two knives. The extra knife would then be worth more than the tunic that I needed to complete my shopping. I could get the tunic only if I were willing to "overpay" by 50 percent or if I could arrange some indirect chain of barters that would leave me holding my "change" in the form of some other commodity.

The second problem is that my pig may be ready for someone else to slaughter or to employ in breeding at a time when my knife is not broken and my tunic is not worn badly. I need to exchange my pig now; but I want to acquire the ability to obtain knives and tunics in the future rather than today. After all, I may need two knives before I need a tunic or two tunics before I need a knife.

Those commodities that are divisible into the smallest units of trading will be possible solutions to the first problem. If a pig sells for three hundred loaves of bread, while knives fetch 150 loaves and tunics go for one hundred each, then I could sell my pig for three hundred, buy one knife and one tunic and keep my change in the form of 50 loaves of bread. This is a poor solution, since I cannot possibly eat 50 loaves before they go stale and I might well not be able to spend them either. An additional inconvenience is that these quantities of bread are very bulky to store and difficult to transport to the vendor of tunics.

Hence, the commodities that begin to function as money, in addition to being divisible into units of small value, will also be relatively imperishable and have high value for a given weight or bulk. Commodities with these characteristics will serve as an admirable solution to the second problem, as well, by retaining their value until needed. Among the goods that meet these criteria, two more qualities are likely to make some superior to others for use as money. First, I would rather keep my change in, or sell my pig for, a commodity that was universally used or valued. Then I could be more confident that I would be able to exchange it for a knife, a tunic, or anything else. Second, I would obviously prefer to obtain a commodity that was also as homogeneously standard and unambiguously recognizable as possible. Otherwise, I might not be certain that I had acquired the specified amount of the genuine article. Even if I had, I may have difficulty in overcoming the subsequent doubts of the knife seller.

Gold and other valuable metals, dried fish, furs, and cigarettes are among the numerous commodities that have served as money in various times and places, because they possessed all of the requisite qualities in varying degrees. That is, they have served as the units in which the value of everything else was measured, as the commodity for which all other commodities were usually exchanged, and finally as the form in which the proceeds of present labor or sales could be stored pending use for future acquisitions.

The oldest evidences we have of money, in the more familiar sense of the precious metals formed into coins, are struck with the images of rulers and the epigrams of governments on the shores of the Aegean Sea in the seventh century before Christ. The first appearance of coinage, the subsequent diversification of denominations, the growth in quantity, and geographic expansion are quite simultaneous with the earliest signs of Greek culture, the ensuing development of that culture, and the expansion first of Greek commerce and military might and then of the Roman Empire, which absorbed Greece.

When everything happens at once, it is difficult to say that some of the things are causes or consequences of others. It is easy to imagine that the relativism reflected in Greek philosophy and sculpture was a prerequisite for the growth of commercial city states trading with people who spoke different languages, held different beliefs, and exchanged commodities in different ratios because of local circumstances. It is equally easy to imagine that carrying out such a commerce might have induced the appreciation of subjective relativity in the rest of Greek culture.

The majority view about this and later episodes in the history of money has been that the growth of commerce caused a demand for money that led to its creation. The record also permits us to suppose that the perfection of commodity-money to the point of minting coins with measured standard contents and a stamp of sovereign guarantee was itself an idea of such power that it opened new roads to trade. From the Athens of the Golden Age to the remnants of the Mediterranean empire a thousand years later, most of the classical world was monetized. In cities things were usually sold for cash. So were slaves. Nonslave labor was usually obtained in exchange for food, housing, and other goods, although cash payments were frequent. Whether money was originally a consequence or a cause of the development of mercantile society, it regulated the tone of development thereafter, as the meter of a poem governs its affect.

The use of money contracted in the Dark Ages with the collapse of classical civilization, but it never disappeared. A revival is apparent by the 900s, in conjunction with the renewal of towns made possible by the increased productivity of feudal agriculture. Once more, the growth in the quantity, complexity, and geographic compass of money was contemporaneous with the great revolutions in culture, science, technology, politics, warfare, commerce, and industry that created the "modern" world.

One of the earliest revolutionary innovations appears in the field of money itself. As early as the time of William the Conqueror and the First Crusade, the quantity of money in the service of trade was mysteriously multiplied by the full-blown appearance of what we now call credit and banking. Starting in Venice, Florence, and other towns of northern Italy, merchants accepted deposits of gold and silver, issuing in return (and for a fee) a piece of paper redeemable for the coins or ingots at the bank. This warehouse receipt was more convenient to transport and safer as well, since it could be rendered as useless to a thief as a stolen credit card is today.

Merchants who specialized in this activity were in fact proprietors of the first modern banks. Many credit transactions far more complicated than the warehouse receipt appeared even earlier in the commerce of Europe as the second millennium began. Typical of these was the bill of exchange. A merchant who anticipated the need to make a payment in the currency of a foreign realm was issued a check by the home office, payable abroad in the desired currency by an office of his own bank or by an office of a local bank.

It is apparent that this substitution of pieces of paper in circulation for equal values of gold in the vaults of banks led immediately to a more glittering possibility. Since the banker's warehouse receipt was not just as good as gold, but even better, it tended to stay in circulation, passing from one business exchange to the next, while the gold stayed in the banker's vault. Receipts were occasionally returned for gold but additional gold was sometimes deposited as well in return for new receipts. So long as ill-fortune, the banker's own greed, or bad judgment did not lessen confidence in his receipts, it was clearly a prudent possibility to issue receipts that were some rational *multiple* of the gold in his bank.

Similarly, the bill of exchange usually made its journey out of the country and returned to the issuing bank for settlement in gold in about as many months as it took the bank's merchant-client to obtain his foreign goods and bring them home for a profitable sale. The bank could issue the bill of exchange to a trusted merchant in consideration of a share of the ultimate profits rather than for an initial deposit of gold and payment of a fee.

An important result of these new institutions was that a given amount of gold in a banker's vault could effect many more business transactions than it would have in circulation as coin. Indeed, in the vault, gold could complete numerous transactions simultaneously and in diverse locations. The true alchemy of the Middle Ages was this transformation of ink and parchment into gold. Ever since that time, the dimensions of our monetary existence have exceeded our material supplies of gold, silver, and other mundane commodities; and the magnitude of this extension has generally increased over the centuries.

This completes an outline of the bare plot of the history of money. German historians in the late 1800s and early 1900s, who were wont to classify everything in its proper category, made this a drama in three great acts: Barter, Money, and Credit. In economic history the value of a classification scheme is not so much whether it enables us to make a positive identification, as does the arrangement in a field guide to birds, but whether it illuminates functions and the process of change, as does the geologist's division of rocks into igneous, sedimentary, and metamorphic.

Just this point was pressed by the critics of the monetary categorization. Behind the veil of money was another sequence of events that dramatically altered the material conditions of human life: the Agricultural Revolution, when people first bred and cultivated animals and crops; and the Industrial Revolution, which expanded human mastery over the environment even more than had its predecessor. The first of these revolutions occurred somewhere in the middle of the many millennia during which humans bartered; and the second occurred about 700 years after the innovation of credit. In other words, the Europe of 1850, with its factories, firearms, and railroads, was vastly different from the Europe of 1350, although both were suffused with credit. While Europe in the fourteenth century was not so different in its physical possessions and industrial arts from Rome a thousand years earlier under the reign of money or Egypt two thousand years before that in the domain of barter.

This technological view of historical epochs has been dominant among economists in recent years, to the extent that they have applied themselves to any question that predates the series of quarterly data following World War II. It sits well in a discipline that is increasingly self-satisfied with its scientific foundations and rational rigor. Nevertheless, the technological view rests on two misperceptions.

The first is a matter of perspective. From the awesome heights of present technology, medieval Europe, ancient Rome, and more ancient Egypt all shrink into similar dots of underdevelopment. We lack adequate statistics to demonstrate differences in income *per capita*. However, we do know that Rome was distinguished from pyramid-building Egypt by domed buildings and keystoned arches; by aqueducts, plumbing, public baths, and widespread protection of public health; and by a vastly increased diversity of goods made possible through Empire-wide roads, navigation, and commerce.

The evidence for a higher standard of living in the monetized Greco-Roman world is partly in the surplus resources that were available for many extensive public works; but it is primarily the vast increase in the quantity and quality of the visual and plastic arts, in poetry and drama, and in philosophy and science that demonstrates a civilization that had moved a giant step further from the exigencies of survival.

The second misperception might be called a failure to penetrate the Veil of Materialism. Economists are as easily fooled into seeing everything as a simply mechanistic relationship between physical quantities as they are skilled at penetrating the disguise of money. The repeated failures in recent decades of more machines and constructions to alter the economic backwardness of many countries and neighborhoods should have restrained this tendency, but it hasn't.

An experimental failure of less immediate practical consequence has had a greater impact on economics. About twenty-five years ago, economists realized that they could not account for actual economic growth with measures of the physical increases in labor, capital, and raw materials. Theory was forced to confront the reality that humans learn to do things more efficiently over the experience of individual lifetimes, organizational lifetimes, and the cumulation of our historical existence. Economists call the fruits of this learning "human capital." Although it has a primarily invisible existence inside our minds, economics treats it as another factor of production, like machinery or petroleum, which can be sold or leased by its owners to consumers or producers. This is a useful fiction for many purposes, including analysis of less-developed regions. In addition, by defining this peculiar new substance, economics can cling to its mechanistic materialism.

There is another and higher dimension in the interaction between intelligence, society, and economics that is not so easily reduced to an exercise like Newtonian physics. From the middle of the 1100s, when the construction of Notre Dame was begun in Paris, to the early 1300s, when Giotto was painting in Italy, Europe experienced an intellectual and economic explosion. Many innovations (for example, the compass) were adopted from other cultures with a skill and enthusiasm similar to that of twentieth-century Japan. The windmill spread rapidly across the continent after its invention and was applied, along with water power, to diverse industrial activities. The determination of inquiry and experiment was best illustrated by the fabulous invention and perfection of the mechanical clock.

All kinds of commerce and production expanded apace. In the conventional view, monetary innovations were a response to this acceleration of real activity. In the actual event, the money prices of things increased by 300 percent over this period. Little or none of this increase can be attributed to the more intense mining of silver. Rather, gold and silver in the coffers of banks was transformed into the equivalent of four times its actual quantity and as much more beyond this as was necessary to keep up with the quickening economic tempo. It appears from this evidence that money was a prime mover of real events, not just a symptom.

It was an age of transcendence. The Gothic cathedral triumphed over space. Rose windows transformed the sun's monochromatic light. The university and the Scholastics broke the bonds of tradition. The chivalric epics of Roland and Arthur provided a new past. People believed in a new future. Our age was born.

The essential accomplishment in each of these examples was a product of the mind or the spirit. So, too, the transcendence of the *idea* of credit over commodities extracted from the earth. There is no reason to suppose that any of these ideas took causal precedence over the others. But there is good reason to conclude that in the narrower realm of economic activity, the new idea of money was of primary importance.

Through what channels did money and credit work their wonders? The mechanical view taken by most economists looked for some efficiencies in the use of scarce materials. Karl Marx emphasized the superiority of bank credit and paper money as economizers of gold, which was a scarce commodity. To obtain the traditional advantages of gold-money versus barter, society had to bear the expense of finding the precious metal, mining it, refining, minting, and reminting it. However, Marx added, "Only insofar as paper money represents gold, which like all other commodities has value, is it a symbol of value." A century earlier, Ben Franklin had pursued the same argument, although he appreciated the ability of paper money and bank credit to augment the stock of precious metals as well as to provide a convenient substitute in actual commerce:

> *Bills of Credit* are found very convenient in Business; because a great Sum is more easily counted in Them, lighter in Carriage, concealed in less Room, and therefore safer in Traveling . . . The Banks are the general Cashiers of all Gentlemen, Merchants, and great Traders . . . there they deposite their Money [i.e., gold and silver coins], and may take out Bills to the Value, for which they can be certain to have Money again at the Bank at any Time . . . And the Bankers always reserving Money in hand to answer more than the common Run of Demands . . . are able besides to lend

large Sums . . . and the Money which otherwise would have lain dead in their Hands, is made to circulate again . . . And thus the Running Cash of the Nation is as it were doubled . . .

The savings on which Marx and Franklin rely—reductions in the costs of coining, mining, and transporting precious metals—seem quite small stuff compared with the economic transformation that followed. The ability to double the monetary effect of a given quantity of gold and silver—in fact, to quadruple it or multiply it by almost any arbitrary number—suggests a force more likely to produce great events.

The ability to manufacture money more cheaply and plentifully than gold can be compared to similar technological advances in the manufacture of other products. The cheap and plentiful good pours out of the new manufacturing centers and floods new markets, as did British textiles in the nineteenth century or Japanese automobiles in more recent times. The period of inflation from the 1100s on was a time of rapid decline in the "price" of money. It took less of any other commodity or labor to "buy" a given amount of money. As its price fell, money invaded many markets that had previously been confined to barter or self-sufficiency. Agriculture was extensively commercialized to feed the growing population of the towns. Craftsmen who had worked exclusively in the domains of lords and bishops were increasingly employed by the money of multiple buyers.

Credit, therefore, was a crucial means by which monetization of the medieval world proceeded further and faster than had the similar transmutation wrought by money alone in the classical world. This still does not tell us anything about why either process of monetization may have had important consequences beyond the most obvious. To answer such a question requires that we penetrate more deeply behind the Veil of Materialism and consider the nature of human personality and social organization.

Societies, before the advent of money, existed in an apparent great variety. The Aztecs and Egyptians—with their extensive domains, public works, articulated division of tasks, and abundant resources—belong in this category along with tribes of

Stone Age hunters and everything in between. Sir John Hicks, the Nobel economist, has proposed two common denominators for this diverse collection. He suggests that in all of them personal behavior was governed by some combination of custom and command. One did either what one was told to do or what everyone else did and had "always" done in like circumstance.

Where there were sailors, hunters, warriors, and others who traveled or where there were those who tried to control the destiny of changing conditions, such as merchants and physicians, there must surely have been a tendency for thought to develop in more independent directions. Such efforts withered, apparently because they require a critical minimum mass to overcome the inertia of custom and command. In part this conclusion can be deduced from the fact that in subsequent history most outstanding independent thought and creativity have occurred in dense clusters within narrow confines of time and geography.

In this context, money defines a distinctly different mode of social organization and personal behavior. It erodes the social structures of custom and command, replacing them with markets. Individual actions become increasingly exchanges of goods and efforts for money or the reverse. These exchanges are the new lifeblood of society. Market rules, conditions, and prices take the place of the commands of chiefs and lords or the dictates of tradition. In many aspects of life, money mediates between persons and between a person and natural reality.

For a society that values change, progress, and accomplishment, this is a fine social system. If a community also wishes to differentiate and exalt the individual rather than the collective, either as a means to its other goals or as an end in itself, markets with money create the only social organization we know that is suitable. At the same time, the sway of money "depersonalizes" our individual and community life and degrades the spontaneity of art and love in ways that have proved disturbing.

The advance of material and intellectual accomplishment in the last eight centuries is enormous by comparison with the progress of the Greco-Roman world in the eight centuries after the introduction of money. It may be that this is due to the more powerful and malleable conception of credit with which we started. However, it is more probable that the superior idea of money was only one aspect of a more exalted determination to master material conditions and expand the limits of thinking without end.

9

The Current
of Progress

In every kingdom into which money begins to flow in
greater abundance than formerly, everything takes on
a new face; labour and industry gain life; the merchant
becomes more enterprising, the manufacturer more dil-
igent and skilful, and even the farmer follows his
plough with greater alacrity and attention.

DAVID HUME
"Of Money" (1752)

For generations, one of the most disrupting junctures in courses
that introduce undergraduates to the principles of economics
has been the moment when students are asked to understand
that and how banks create new money. Initial disbelief is grudg-
ingly dispelled as students dutifully make their way through
double-entry bookkeeping for banks: Your debt to the bank is
the bank's asset and the balance in your checking account is the
bank's liability. Everything balances and the balance is stable so
long as enough of the bank's assets can be turned back into cash
with sufficient speed to satisfy occasional fluctuations in the
desires of its depositors to cash checks or write checks that end
up being deposits in a different bank. Students are further mol-
lified upon learning that the process of money creation is mercifully complex so that even the banker who makes a loan is
unaware of the fact that he is creating money. At this point,
most classes can be divided into two camps—those who think
this is the neatest trick they have been taught since logarithms,
and those who think it is a sleight of hand that is too quick to
penetrate and definitely immoral.

In the early years of the Industrial Revolution, men of learning and experience were similarly divided. We have already seen that Franklin thought banking was a straightforward and practical business with wonderfully beneficent effects. Franklin had no doubt that money was a concretely real thing, a commodity like gold or silver whose value was determined in the same fashion as any other commodity. The notes of bankers and the drafts of their customers were good only because they were as good as the real thing. There was no more disagreement about this already false proposition in the late 1700s and early 1800s than there is among students in today's Economics 1 classroom about to hear how banks create money.

In 1776, Adam Smith was the lecturer. In the first volume of *The Wealth of Nations* he looked at the manufacture of money under the dispassionate lens of Scotch rationality:

> A particular banker lends among his customers his own promissory notes, to the extent, we shall suppose, of a hundred thousand pounds. As those notes serve all the purposes of money, his debtors pay him the same interest as if he had lent them so much money . . . Though some of those notes are continually coming back upon him for payment, part of them continue to circulate for months and years together. Though he has generally in circulation, therefore, notes to the extent of a hundred thousand pounds, twenty thousand pounds in gold and silver may frequently be a sufficient provision for answering occasional demands . . . Twenty thousand pounds in gold and silver perform all the functions which a hundred thousand could otherwise have performed.

Smith is at some pains for many pages before and after this statement to demonstrate the skill, prudence, and integrity required of the banker who would draw such rabbits out of his hat.

When John Adams read this passage, he concluded, "Every dollar of a bank bill that is issued beyond the quantity of gold and silver in the vaults represents nothing and is therefore a cheat upon somebody." The choice of words is curious, suggesting that despite his Puritan disapproval, his wide knowledge of commercial practices, and his immense intelligence, it was not quite clear to Adams *who* was being cheated by this evident fraud.

Adam Smith did not trouble himself with such questions; at least not in his writings. Perhaps it seemed clear to him that the principal victims of such practices would be those who initially had something approaching a monopoly on money, wealth, and property: the landed aristocracy and other remnants of a feudal order that was being replaced by the new wealth and liberty proclaimed from Glascow and Geneva, Paris and Philadelphia. Thus, Smith concentrates instead on his favorite point. In typically plodding prose, he sets forth his immediately appealing argument that although the rabbits are first pulled out of the hat to benefit the magician, nevertheless their continued existence is a great general benefit to society. The benefits explained by Smith were much the same as those listed by Franklin or for that matter in the 1600s by William Petty. Society would be saved much of the expense of finding, producing, and minting gold in order to have the money that it required.

By implication, the answer that Adam Smith would have given to John Adams is that since no one owned the rabbit before it existed no one can be said to have been robbed by its creation. Furthermore, since the rabbit hopped perpetually from person to person, its creation cannot be said to have conferred special advantage on the first recipient to the relative detriment of others. The borrower, after all, exchanged his promise to pay with interest for the money, just as subsequent members of the chain exchanged their goods or efforts for the same money. Competition among borrowers and among bankers would ensure that money created for borrowers would go for the most productive purposes, with the highest chance of being paid back and at the lowest possible interest cost.

Smith left the statement and elaboration of these themes to his nineteenth- and twentieth-century followers. He goes immediately ahead to a natural question. If the requisite money supply already exists fully in the form of gold, what is the consequence of having the bankers start to turn every gold coin into the foundation for five times as much paper money? In one of his more credulous or disingenuous passages, Smith explains that the proper total amount of money will not change. Therefore, one fifth of the circulating gold will disappear into banks.

The banks will issue as much paper to circulate as there had been gold circulating. The remaining four fifths of the original gold will become redundant as money. It will therefore be available to society as a whole to make jewelry or to buy things of more irreplaceable value from less enlightened countries.

I think the contemporary monetarists and advocates of laissez-faire capitalism who describe themselves as disciples of Adam Smith would, nevertheless, offer the following interpretation of Smith's analysis. Adam was advocating a flood of printing-press money to help his industrialist friends build new factories. He knew the resulting inflation would effectively penalize the aristocrats, thus forcing them by an almost invisible arm twist to subsidize his capitalist buddies. The inflation would also make British goods less attractive to foreigners and foreign goods more in demand in Britain. Hence, money would flow out of Britain. Under the principles formulated by Thomas Gresham during the reign of Queen Elizabeth I, the flood of new paper money would drive the more valuable gold money out of circulation. Just as Adam Smith said, all of the gold would go into the vaults of foreigners or banks, leaving only the paper money in circulation.

For most conservatives, Gresham's Law has been a caution against unleashing floods of cheap money. For the revolutionary, Adam Smith, in his zeal against those who confused gold with labor and the fruits of labor, which were the true wealth of nations, there was every reason to throw caution to the winds. *The Wealth of Nations* and the American War of Independence appeared simultaneously. The American Revolution created what may have been the most explosive inflation from the end of Thomas Gresham's 1500s until the end of World War I. The Revolution was fought against an imperial system that was properly scathed by Adam Smith. Nevertheless, the American inflation bore little resemblance to the situation that Smith described.

The new paper money was not issued by private banks but by the Continental Congress and the thirteen self-proclaimed new states. Essentially, none of these governments had *any* gold with which to redeem their notes; nor did they usually make any promise to redeem them. The money was not spent to build new factories. It was used to finance a life-or-death military struggle. This was sufficient reason to behave incautiously. The resulting American inflation painfully burned an impression in the minds of participants and observers that can be comprehended in our own time only by analogy with the deep impact that the German inflation after World War I has had on twentieth-century thought.

When the Revolutionary Congress first issued its paper money in 1775, it took about $1.50 to buy what one Spanish silver dollar would purchase. By 1781, the rebellious states were suffering from the weight of over $400 million of paper money issued by the Congress and the states (the equivalent with today's population and income levels would be the issuance of $4 trillion of new paper money in six years). As a result it took one hundred Continental dollars to buy what could be obtained with one Spanish silver dollar. Hence the expression "Not worth a Continental." At the same time, the Revolution drew resources out of the production of food and manufactured goods and brought additional French, German, and English troops to America, all demanding more goods. Therefore, even in Spanish dollars or British Pounds Sterling, the price level in America tripled during the same six years. What cost $1.50 Continental Currency in 1775 cost $300 in the early 1780s, or two hundred times as much. Even in Britain, this early imperial police action drove the gold and silver prices of things up by about 40 percent.

Like all the important events of his time, this devastating inflation drew the attention of Benjamin Franklin. After an accurate history of the paper-money finance of the Revolution, in which he details the limited possibilities for borrowing gold and silver money from France and Holland—negotiations in which Franklin himself played a central role—and the limited possibilities for imposing taxes on a divided American populace, of whom the most militant revolutionaries were protesting the imposition of British taxes, Franklin offers the following analysis:

> The general effect of the depreciation [of the Continental currency] among the inhabitants of the States has been this, that it has operated as a *gradual tax* upon them, their business has been done and paid for by the paper money, and every man has paid his share of the tax according to the time he retained any of the money in his hands, and to the depreciation within that time. Thus it has proved a tax on money, a kind of property very difficult to be taxed in any other mode; and it has fallen more equally than many other taxes, as those people paid most, who, being richest, had most money passing through their hands.

The basic insight that inflation caused by the issue of government paper is a tax upon money is now accepted by all economists. Franklin's explicit endorsement of this tax as particularly efficacious and just has been implicitly accepted by innumerable left-leaning regimes in the subsequent two centuries.

Indeed, Franklin was a true precursor of many modern "Keynesians." He preferred growth and full employment to stagnation and idleness. He saw more money as the means of achieving the preferred circumstances and inflation as a small price to pay for such achievements. He cared little whether the money was created by bankers or governments or whether it was backed by precious metals, farmers' land, solemn pledges, or specious promises. He loved the excitement of an economic boom no less than amorous pursuits or scientific inquiry.

The architect of the Franklin stove and flyer of kites in thunderstorms was too much a man of this earth to concern himself with the philosophical essence of money. Clearly, gold and silver were just commodities whose relative prices fluctuated with demand and supply, the same as tobacco or wool. The essence of money was not its metallic content. Money was defined by its *function,* and its function was to enable the multilateral exchange of produce, disjointed in time, to replace the immediate bilateral barter of shoes for wheat. For Franklin and Smith, money was the water whose currents carried the exciting flow of goods. The labor and energy of production and the wealth of consumption were the substantive attributes of economic activity to be admired and encouraged. Money was like the ether of physics before Michelson, Morley, and Einstein, an insensible medium through which heat, light, and gravity were transmitted. Franklin would no more have praised or analyzed the material essence of money than he would the void between the heavenly spheres.

It was from this intelligent tradition of the ethereal essence of money that the nineteenth century found the basis of its episodic contempt for the pursuit of money *qua* money. From Charles Dickens to Thomas Hardy the pathology of the money grubber was ridiculed. From Karl Marx to Sigmund Freud the delusion of his fetishism was exposed.

Some of the earliest and most sour disapprovals of money were written by Thomas Jefferson. The slave-owning Virginia planter was as Puritanical as any Massachusetts lawyer or farmer. In 1816 he wrote,

> Like a dropsical man calling out for water, water, our deluded citizens are clamoring for more banks, more banks . . . We are now taught to believe that legerdemain tricks upon paper can produce as solid wealth as hard labor in the earth. It is vain for common sense to urge that *nothing* can produce but *nothing;* that it is an idle dream to believe in a philosopher's stone which is to turn everything into gold.

For Jefferson, it was a violation of his rationalist faith to suppose that anyone might actually have performed a true magic trick, let alone that the trick should have been perfected in the Europe of absolute monarchs and religions. Two centuries ago it was transparent to both friend and foe of banks that they literally created money—a point that one might spend the better part of a semester conveying to a class of skeptical undergraduates. For Jefferson and Adams, the issue was not so much ontology as morality. Money *ought* to be as difficult to manufacture as the goods that it could purchase. For Jefferson, the suspension of common sense that induced people to trade their goods and labor for mere scraps of paper was a form of delusional hysteria, as dangerous and immoral as all other speculative excesses. For Smith and Franklin, the possession of money was inconsequential compared to the valuable functions that it performed for all of society as the universal medium of commercial

exchange. If more of the stuff could be created without the difficulty and uncertainty of finding and mining precious metals,
then we were all the beneficiaries of this bounty.

From Jefferson through the last of the Jacksonian Democrats
there persisted a curious inversion of the traditional alignment
of political forces on money questions. The parties of popular
democracy and economic equality were inaptly the advocates
of "hard" money. Unlike Ben Franklin before, or William Jennings Bryan after, they *did* want to crucify the country on a
cross of gold. In part this was because the Democratic Party of
Andrew Jackson was no more a pure congregation of the poor
and homeless than the Democratic Party of Lyndon Johnson.
Often, hostile acts toward particular banking institutions and
practices had the intent or the effect of benefiting those banks
and locations that supported the incumbent Democrats.

Those who wanted more banks and more money were those
who also wanted more roads, canals, factories, commerce, population, and wealth. Money was a means to these ends. Indeed,
many of the leading advocates of these policies had emerged
from obscurity or secondary rank to positions of wealth and
power because of the tumult and inflation of the Revolution.
Then as now, banks lent money to people who didn't have
enough of it for their purposes, and not to those who had practically none of it. The borrower's purpose was often manufacturing or trade, sometimes to clear and improve new land in Mis-
sissippi and to purchase slaves from Virginia to work it, less
often to buy stock in a bridge, canal, turnpike, railroad, or
another bank.

Therefore, the immediate effect of pulling more rabbits out of
the hat was to bestow upon the borrowers more merchandise at
sea, more factories, plantations, canals, and so on. The injustice
from the point of view of the Jeffersonians was that these benefits were often more durable than the rabbit. As Jefferson argued in his 1816 letter, the issuance and acceptance of paper
money by banks tended to expand in speculative bubbles that
were bound to burst, leaving the last holder of bank notes as
cheated as the bag holders of Continental Currency at the end
of the Revolution. Jefferson's vision was realized only three

years later in the panic of 1819. Substantial amounts of bank notes and deposits became worthless (including some held by Andrew Jackson). Massive bank failures occurred again in the period 1837 through 1843, at various times after the Civil War through 1907, and most recently and gigantically in the Great Depression.

Here was a pretty clear identification of the "somebody" upon whom John Adams claimed the banks' creation of money was "a cheat." Many somebodies were left afoot with worthless money in this game of musical chairs. Meanwhile, the original borrowers were lords of their new estates, and the bank owners (who were often much the same group as the borrowers) often went unscathed, because they had put little capital into the banks in the first place and there had been profits to make before the music stopped.

10

A Fearsome
Imagination

So, first of all, let me assert my firm belief that the only
thing we have to fear is fear itself . . . our distress
comes from no failure of substance. We are stricken by
no plague of locusts . . . Nature still offers her bounty
and human efforts have multiplied it. Plenty is at our
doorstep, but a generous use of it languishes in the very
sight of the supply. Primarily this is because rulers of
the exchange of mankind's goods have failed through
their own stubbornness and their own incompetence,
have admitted their failure, and have abdicated. Practices of the unscrupulous money changers stand in-
dicted in the court of public opinion, rejected by the
hearts and minds of men.

True they have tried, but their efforts have been cast
in the pattern of an outworn tradition. Faced by failure
of credit they have proposed only the lending of more
money . . .

Happiness lies not in the mere possession of money;
it lies in the joy of achievement, in the thrill of
creative effort.

FRANKLIN DELANO ROOSEVELT
Inaugural Address (1933)

From the beginning, a majority of American political opinion
has rejected the notion that money was a game of musical chairs
for some inherent reason, rather than because of a mere shortage of chairs, or surplus of players, that could be remedied by
public policy. The creation of the Federal Reserve Bank in
1913, in the aftermath of the severe panic of 1907, was intended to provide such a public remedy. Its preamble stated
that the Federal Reserve Act was intended "To provide for the

establishment of Federal reserve banks, to furnish an elastic currency, to afford means of rediscounting commercial paper, to establish a more effective supervision of banking in the United States, and for other purposes." The key phrase was "to furnish an elastic currency," everything else being viewed as means to this end.

The problem in 1907 (as well as 1893, 1873, 1857, 1837, and 1819) had been that the holders of claims on money wanted to cash them in for the real thing. But there were more claims than there was of whatever it was people wanted to turn them into. That, after all, was the whole point of the game. Not only did the idea of claims, in the form of bank deposits or bank notes, supplant the use of "real" money in circulation; but, over time, the idea of what the real money was also changed. In 1819, depositors and note holders mostly wanted the gold and silver coins of England or Spain, although many would have been happy with the notes issued by the strong and semipublic Second Bank of the United States. By 1907, almost all of the anxious depositors who formed lines at the tellers' windows only wanted to convert their checkbook balances into one of the various kinds of green paper that passed for money. This paper, which was viewed as the real thing, included the notes of the very banks whose depositors were panicked.

If all that had to be done to supply everyone with a chair when the music stopped was to provide more green paper, this seemed simple enough compared to the unpleasant consequences of permitting the banking system to freeze up. What was needed was only a method of making the supply of paper currency "elastic," so that more of it would be available whenever the public feared for the safety of its deposits, setting off a competition among worried banks and their customers to possess more of the fixed supply of cash (or whenever the pace of business expanded for seasonal or cyclical reasons).

These powers were given to the Federal Reserve System. The new central bank was equipped to carry out the various maneuvers that private banks had developed to deal with the periodic crises that struck individual banks or swept the entire system. Now these expedients had the blessing of the federal government, and their administration was entrusted to an authority that could act swiftly and decisively. If need be, the Federal Reserve can purchase all of the assets (loans and securities) of any bank and print an equal quantity of its own Federal Reserve notes to pay for them. Since these notes *are* the money that depositors expect to be able to draw from their accounts, the Federal Reserve can insure the equivalence of checking accounts and cash, so long as banks are supervised to make sure that they do not steal their depositors' money or squander it on worthless assets.

Less than twenty-five years after the Federal Reserve was created, the United States experienced the most extensive and prolonged collapse of money, credit, and banks in its entire history. From the summer of 1929 to the spring of 1933, one out of every five banks in the country was unable to meet its obligations and had to close; one out of every ten dollars in checking and savings accounts was momentarily or permanently extinguished; the nation's total money supply declined by about one third. In the end, every single bank in the country was closed, and all functions were suspended for a week. The remedy that had been provided in 1913 to deal with exactly such a problem did not ameliorate the crisis, primarily because those charged with administering it failed to do so.

As a consequence of this failure, the structure of public legislation was extended considerably in the early days of the New Deal to ensure not only that there would be plenty of chairs the next time the music stopped, but that someone would certainly whisk them into place as well. The Federal Home Loan Bank was created to serve as a lender of last resort for savings institutions, just as the Federal Reserve did for commercial banks. The Federal Deposit Insurance Corporation provided an entirely new and independent defense for the integrity of bank deposits and a new and independent authority for additional supervision of bank practices. The deference of the original Federal Reserve Act to regional autonomy was sacrificed for a more centralized structure of decision and command.

A major weapon was added to the Fed's arsenal. Previously, the Fed had been able to create new money by purchasing (or "rediscounting") the assets of any particular bank that needed additional liquidity to satisfy its depositors or to maintain adequate reserves. The terms on which such assistance is offered can effectively discipline the money-creating behavior of individual banks. The Fed has also always had the ability to create new money by purchasing U.S. government bonds or any other asset for its own account and paying with newly created purchasing power. Similarly, it can decrease the amount of such money in the system by reversing the procedure and selling securities that it already owns for money, which it permits to disappear from circulation. The amount of money supplied or withdrawn by these "open market" activities disciplines the ability of all banks collectively to create additional money.

The original Federal Reserve Act had specified the amount of reserves, mostly in the form of Federal Reserve notes and deposits, that national banks were required to maintain against different kinds of their own deposits. Since these reserves are the kind of money that the Federal Reserve creates when it purchases assets from individual banks or in the open market, these legislative ratios determine the leveraged impact of a given Fed move on the money supply. The additional weapon given to the Fed by the New Deal Banking Acts was the ability to set and to vary the reserve ratios themselves. Since then, the Fed has been able to make and change the rules that set finite limits on the potentially infinite multiplicative magic of money creation.

Nor was all this the end of reforms. Most activities of commercial banking (holding deposits and making loans) were segregated by statute from the activities of investment banking (acting as a broker, a dealer, or an underwriter of stocks and bonds). Banks were prohibited from paying interest on demand deposits and the interest they could pay on savings accounts was subjected to regulation. Because of the particularly critical role of speculation in the stock market, followed by the Great Crash, bank lending that was secured by stocks and bonds was brought under a whole complex of regulatory rules and procedures.

These responses to the 1929–1933 disaster were substantially redundant. Federal Deposit Insurance has proved to be a powerful, double-edged sword, more than sufficient to maintain the solvency of bank deposits all by itself. On the one side, insurance does this quite directly up to the amount of coverage on every deposit. On the other side, by increasing public confidence, insurance has stifled the periodic outbreaks of panic that were self-fulfilling in earlier times.

There has thus been no occasion for the streamlined Federal Reserve to employ its enhanced powers to forestall a run on the banks as it had failed to do in the Great Depression. Indeed, the last fifty years have been marked by unprecedented calm and stability. Over the past forty years an average of five banks (mostly small) have failed each year throughout the country. (The year 1982 was a dismal exception to this record.) This compares with the total of sixteen thousand banks that failed during the years 1900–1933, including some of the largest ones. On average, twice as many banks failed every year in the earlier period as the total number that closed in the past four decades. While depositors bore all of the loss involved in earlier closings, once the owners of the bank were wiped out, insurance has compensated them for the lion's share of losses ever since.

For the first thirty years, the Federal Reserve earnestly employed its new ability to periodically adjust required reserve ratios against deposits. Since the mid-1960s it has changed them less frequently and has relied instead on its ability to change the quantity of reserves available to banks.

The remaining innovations of the 1930s have been steadily eroded or evaded over the last two decades. This deterioration has simultaneously enfeebled the control of the Federal Reserve and reduced the effective coverage of insurance. Our ability to sustain the superior record of nearly half a century is now in question.

The attempt to separate commercial banking from dealing in stocks and bonds may have had some merit on various grounds, but not as a direct remedy for the systemic failure of banking during the Depression. The stock market mania of the 1920s had only provided one of many opportunities for impulsive and inexperienced managers to ruin their banks. In any case, the imprudence of individual banks and the thievery of individual bankers does not appear to have been any more common in 1929 than it is today, nor to have been a major cause of the debacle. It can be noted, without particular concern, that banks always retained an interest in securities markets as owners of bonds for their own portfolios and managers of stock and bond investments for others through their trust departments. Over time, the trust departments have gained importance in securities markets, largely because their competitors (brokers and investment management companies) were subject to much more restrictive regulation under the Securities and Exchange Commission than the trust departments encountered under various bank regulators. In addition, the role of banks has gradually expanded, with the help of bank holding companies and new legislation, into more aspects of securities trading and underwriting. To the extent that these activities are independent of the lending and investing of depositors' money they are little threat to the solvency of banks. By the same token, they should be of little concern to the federal and state agencies that govern bank behavior. They ought, more properly and equitably, to be supervised by the Securities and Exchange Commission, as are their nonbank competitors.

The prohibition of interest payments on demand deposits and the imposition of interest-rate ceilings on time deposits belong to that vast universe of price-fixing schemes that have always been favored by politicians and scorned by economists. Others include agricultural price supports and rent controls. If such prohibitions and ceilings have any effect, they must benefit banks, and/or those who borrow from banks, at the expense of depositors who supply the money. As price increases accelerated over the years since 1933, so did the inflation tax on no-interest and low-interest deposits of money. The resulting pressure led to the creation of various ways in which banks were able to pay interest on demand accounts and to pierce interest-rate ceilings when they began to bind.

First came the Certificate of Deposit (CD) in the late 1950s. In effect, a bank borrows money from someone (usually a corporation) for a specified length of time and agrees to pay the free market rate of interest for loans rather than the regulated maximum for deposits. The lender receives a certificate specifying the amount of the loan, the interest, and the maturity date. The certificate is negotiable. That is, the lender can sell the note from the bank to someone else before it matures. Because the borrower is a bank, and because the bank chooses to call its debt a Certificate of *Deposit,* the CD takes on the acceptability and liquidity of money itself. Another rabbit out of the hat.

The Federal Reserve responded halfheartedly to this decisive breach of the intent of the Banking Acts by restricting CD's to minimum amounts of $100,000 and minimum terms of thirty days. This response resulted in part from the conviction of economists at the central bank that interest-rate ceilings on deposits were not a good idea anyway and in part from the tendency of the Federal Reserve, like all regulatory agencies, to promote the interests of its flock rather than to constrain them.

Inevitably, a swarm of innovations appeared to devour the remaining crumbs of original legislative restraint. The money market funds take cash from those of us who deal in amounts under $100,000, reinvest our pooled funds in bank CD's, and provide the public with high interest rates and the ability to write checks. You don't even have to be a bank (and therefore regulated as such) to produce money by "legerdemain tricks upon paper."

Meanwhile, banks have been permitted to offer various mini-CD's that pay close to market rates for various sizes and maturities under the original barriers. The NOW account is nothing but a plain demand account on which banks pay interest. Its name, Negotiable Order of Withdrawal, only reflects its origin as an attempt to submerge the obviously illegal thing it was by wrapping it in a different name. Because money is principally an idea, the naming of monetary concepts has played a substantive role in history.

Banks developed an additional tool for evading the Federal Reserve's 30-day-minimum-maturity requirement for CD's. In this case, a new employment was developed for an old device, the Repurchase Agreement. Under a Repurchase Agreement, the owner of a security sells it to someone else and simultaneously agrees to repurchase it at a fixed date (typically a day to a few weeks in the future) and a fixed price calculated to provide the second party with a reasonable rate of interest. In effect, the owner of the security pawns it for a few days in order to borrow funds. This device has been used for centuries by securities dealers as a way of using their inventories to obtain needed cash or their cash to obtain needed inventory. In recent years, commercial banks rapidly expanded their use of Repurchase Agreements with the general public as a way of using their securities portfolios to bid for funds at competitive interest rates while avoiding the 30-day limit, the $100,000 limit, or both.

As a result of these developments, banks pay interest for most of the funds they obtain, and they pay more interest than they used to for most categories of funds. Indeed, they are now permitted to offer Money Market Deposit Accounts that are modeled directly after the money market funds. The classic argument against tolerating such a state of affairs was this: If all of the deposits that banks can acquire cost heavy interest payments, then profit-maximizing banks will be neither willing nor able to tolerate investing those funds at anything less than a positive premium over their cost. In particular, banks will be justifiably reluctant to maintain noninterest-earning cash in their vaults (or deposits with the Federal Reserve) just to satisfy the fluctuating demands of their depositors. Similarly, they will be reluctant to maintain investments in U.S. government securities and other assets that can be readily converted into needed cash, if such assets earn little or no premium over the cost of deposits while direct loans, which are difficult to turn into cash, earn more.

Milton Friedman and numerous others with boundless faith in the ability of ungoverned and voracious competition to temper destabilizing forces have held that these concerns were fallacious. Indeed, they are planted by bankers eager to profit from the bounty of interest-free deposits. As is the case with distressing frequency, the logic of economics is impeccable and the evidence of experience is contrary. As a matter of fact, the proportion of total bank deposits that was placed by banks in relatively illiquid loans regained the ill-fated peak levels of 1907 and 1929 around 1970. Since then, this ratio has pushed erratically higher to successive new records. At the same time, the borrowing public has absorbed the cost of higher payments to the depositing public as interest rates on bank loans have been pulled increasingly above interest rates on U.S. government obligations and other nonbank borrowing.

If you interpret these observations as an urgent call to rush to the bank and convert your deposit into dollar bills, you have misread me. As already noted, the structure of banking safeguards erected after the Great Depression was richly redundant. To date, only supports that are superfluous have been abandoned. The entire domestic banking structure still rests solidly on the pillar of Federal Deposit Insurance. However, even if the banking system remains well protected from the panics and failures of earlier epochs, it is still clear that each of these developments has had the effect of making the definition of money more problematic and its control by the Federal Reserve more uncertain.

The most profound monetary innovation of recent decades was a response to different attempts at regulation. In the early 1960s, the United States began to experience serious deficits in its balance of payments. More dollars left the United States than came into it as a result of trade and investments. The administration of John Kennedy addressed this problem by restricting the abilities of corporations and banks to expatriate dollars. One of the proximate causes of the balance of payments deficit was the international expansion of American corporations. Many U.S. companies perceived their domestic profits and markets to be flagging. (See chapter 4.) They were intent on continuing the pursuit of sales and profits overseas. Their bankers were pressured to continue making loans to finance the construction of new foreign facilities and to bolster the finances of new foreign customers.

From this ferment the Eurodollar was brewed. The Voluntary Foreign Credit Restriction Program (in which the word *voluntary* is to be construed strictly in the Orwellian sense) may have constrained lending by Chase Manhattan in New York to IBM in New York; but if Chase Manhattan's foreign subsidiary in London or Frankfurt was able to lend dollars to IBM, the same purpose could be accomplished without violating government restrictions. In the first instance, after the loan was granted, IBM could write dollar checks on its newly created deposit at Chase Manhattan in London.

The Eurodollars thus created were not really a new phenomenon. A Eurodollar is simply a deposit in dollars with a bank that is domiciled outside of the United States and its possessions. The term has too much geographic specificity. A more apt description would be Expatriatedollar or Fritz Machlup's succinct Xenodollar. What was new in the early 1960s was that banks, mostly the foreign subsidiaries of American banks, began to create vast quantities of Eurodollars. By one measure, their supply increased from about $5 billion in 1961 to $65 billion in 1971 and over $900 billion by early 1982. If these amounts are added to a broad and roughly comparable measure of the domestic money supply (M-3), Eurodollars caused this composite money supply to grow about one percent a year faster in the first decade and about two percent faster in the second. If one believes the monetarist gospel of inflation, then Eurodollars have accounted for about one quarter of the inflation that we have experienced in the last twenty years.

The inflationary implications of this growth are significant, but the threat to a safe and reliable monetary system is far greater. The Federal Reserve Bank and the central banks of other countries have elected not to extend their supervisory authority to the Eurobanking system. Eurocurrency deposits are not insured by any private or government institution. No one requires Eurobanks to maintain a level of reserves against their deposits. It is arguable that the entire system has no reserves. Each bank tends to count as reserves its deposits with other banks. While such a system serves very well to smooth fluctuations in the inflows and outflows among banks, it would be of no avail if there were a general desire of depositors to withdraw funds from the whole system.

In such an eventuality, the largest banks, which hold the bulk of "reserve" deposits from other banks, expect to be able to draw more dollars (or whatever other currency is required) from their home offices. However, the Federal Reserve and other central banks have no obligation or commitment to advance funds to Eurobanks or to purchase their assets in order to meet a classic liquidity squeeze. The prophets of perfect competition are enamored with the Eurobanks for precisely these reasons. Here is a system entirely regulated by the rigors of competition; restrained not by government edicts and central bank discipline, but by the perfect modulation of the desire to survive and profit in a sea of competition.

On closer examination one finds there is nothing about this ship that makes it more leakproof than its numerous predecessors, which sank ignominiously in previous centuries. In the beginning, loans were made mostly to multinational corporations to finance new plants or to their customers to finance the purchase of their products. The multinationals have repaid their loans with the profits earned on their new facilities. The customers have not been so fortunate. The typical borrower was a developing country. The borrowed funds were often employed to purchase military hardware, police department computers, showcase steel mills, airports, fleets of aircraft, and various other collections of stuff that was fated from the beginning to be unable to earn economic returns sufficient to repay the principal or interest on the loans.

In the 1970s the OPEC price increases created an enormous need for the same developing countries to borrow enough dollars to maintain their oil imports, which had suddenly become vastly more expensive than the revenues produced by exports. The Eurodollar system kept the international flow of goods going in approximately the same quantities and thereby averted an enormous disaster. Nevertheless, it should be apparent that a country that borrows dollars to import the same oil that it previously could pay for with its exports will not have spent the loan proceeds for any purpose that will enable it to repay the loan.

The resulting system can be caricatured with surprisingly little distortion as follows: Over half the deposits in the system belong to a few dozen multinational corporations and OPEC countries. At first, the American multinationals kept their revenues in Eurodollar deposits because U.S. regulations discouraged the repatriation of dollars earned from the sale of computers or aircraft. When the price of oil was increased, OPEC countries like Saudi Arabia experienced dollar inflows that greatly exceeded their ability or need to spend for imports. This excess was deposited in the Eurodollar banks.

Over half the loans are also owed by a few dozen borrowers. The countries that borrowed in the 1960s to buy petrochemical plants and planes for their national airlines were, not surprisingly, the very same countries who were forced to borrow heavily in the 1970s to pay for petroleum imports. To a large extent, these borrowers—countries like Poland, Spain, Brazil, Mexico, and Indonesia—are unable to repay their loans. Over half of the loans and deposits in the system are held again by a small number of the world's largest banks. When the borrowers are unable to repay, these banks follow the traditional line of least resistance, lending the debtors enough money to repay their loans with interest. And when the new loan is equally played out, yet another loan can be provided.

Thus, a few dozen borrowers owe about $600 billion that they cannot repay. This amount increases by about $60 billion each year through interest alone, not to mention additional credits. The few dozen banks to whom this enormous sum is owed have now grown accustomed to lending additional sums regularly to their impecunious clients so that the original debts can be marked as paid. A few dozen oil-exporting countries and giant multinational corporations hold the same $600 billion of total deposits in the Eurobank system. The value of these deposits also grows by about $60 billion each year through the interest earned by the depositors. Because there are so few players in this game, each can have a clear picture of the entire situation. If the depositors do not demand their money from the banks, then the banks needn't demand their money from the borrowers. So long as the banks rollover their loans and the depositors rollover their deposits everyone is happy. The borrowers continue to enjoy their airplanes, computers, or tanks without being compelled to make any real sacrifice. The banks report rapidly growing loan portfolios with splendid collection records, as well as rapidly growing deposits and profits. The depositors report a bundle of supremely safe deposits with the world's best-known banks, which are earning extraordinary interest as well.

A brief contemplation will reveal that the stability of this structure depends on the continued stability and rationality of its hundred or so principal players. A passing familiarity with history, human nature, or current events will suggest that this splendid construction has the permanence of a sand castle.

The major argument that has been offered as a defense for the failure of the Federal Reserve to impose regulation and reserve requirements on Eurobanking has been that such restraints would merely place foreign subsidiaries of American banks at a competitive disadvantage against their unregulated rivals. Central bankers in America and elsewhere who make this argument must in fact agree with the traditional view that competition is a better regulator than they are. It requires no great intelligence to see that a set of reserve requirements and safeguards that were uniformly applied to all of the Eurobanks by all of the major central banks would leave the competing banks on exactly the same relative footing that they presently enjoy. If some foreign central banks are so myopically attached to the immediate profitability of their countries' private banks that they refuse to cooperate in a common effort at regulation and protection, that is still no reason for the others not to go ahead. Otherwise, they would be like the crew of a listing ship who refused to man the pumps because a recalcitrant and inebriated few had chosen to drink instead of pump.

In August 1982, the Federal Reserve Bank *did* intervene forcefully when Mexico, one of the dozen major borrowers in the Eurocurrency system, was unable to borrow enough new money to pay principal and interest on the $60 billion of debt already outstanding. Other central banks, international monetary institutions, and the Reagan administration were successfully enlisted in the effort. While the imminent bankruptcy of Mexico was certainly not good news, the prompt response of the Federal Reserve *was* good news. And so was the willingness of the Reagan administration to indulge in a "quick fix" after it had so vehemently denounced the concept. One of the sharpest stock market rallies of all time began when news of the Mexican difficulties and the Federal Reserve response became available. The second boost to that rally occurred in October 1982, when the Federal Reserve quite openly abandoned its policy commitment to monetarism. Preventing the collapse of the system from a chain of defaults only deals with half of the problem. It is still necessary to provide adequate new credit to finance a healthy and growing world trade.

It is my earnest hope that by now the reader is convinced that money is important and that money is an idea. Precisely because money is a creation of human imagination, it is subject to the control of human thought and human institutions. The power to create and destroy money and to honor or renounce debts is a power to transfer real resources from one group of individuals to another. For just those reasons, we are obliged to harness the idea of money to the service of a bountiful and equitable distribution of economic benefits.

One of the least thoughtful attempts to redirect the forces of money creation is represented by the proposal to reduce money to gold once again. The genie cannot be so easily stuffed back into the bottle. At recent prices, even at the lofty peak price of nearly $1000 an ounce, all the gold in the world is not worth as much as all the dollars in the world, let alone the money that parades under different flags. Besides, ideas are immortal. Even if dollar bills and bank deposits were as good as gold, nothing could prevent me from selling you my car for your IOU. In a flash, everyone's IOU's, which were definitely not as good as gold, would begin to function as substitutes for the money that was.

Hooking money back up to gold would be a poor idea even if the genie were laid to rest. Our recent inflation would be replicated whenever plentiful new supplies of gold were discovered and exploited, say on the moon or under the oceans. If we learned to make gold inexpensively abundant through some nuclear transmutation, and if gold were also money, then the money price of everything else would rise. The modest benefits of such a scientific advance would be transformed into a debilitating inflation.

Conversely, if gold were found to be an essential component in photovoltaic cells that produced all of our energy from the sun thirty years hence, gold would become more scarce and valuable because of this important new employment. The quantity in banks and coins would decline as the quantity in the useful work of generating the world's energy increased. Again, if gold were money, this otherwise happy discovery would produce an economic catastrophe, as the supply of money disappeared and the gold-money price of everything else plunged.

The clamor for reifying money as gold is only the grossest example of the current idolatry that obscures intelligent perception and hard choices.

PART III

Time and Tide

11

The Pendulum

The only cause of depression is prosperity.

CLEMENT JUGLAR
*Commercial Crises and
Their Periodic Recurrence in France,
in England, and in America* (1862)

What if economic history just repeats itself? For whatever reasons, periods of rising and falling prices or high and low employment may alternate in a majestic cycle. The high unemployment of the 1970s and the worse experience of the early 1980s might represent the inexorable unfolding of this cycle. Perhaps many of the immediate events that we cite as causes and the policies that we prescribe as cures are irrelevant. This would be the case if the true causes of our misfortunes lay prior to recent history or beyond the economic system as we understand it.

I have utilized such ideas in previous parts of this book. The experience of the Great Depression still imparted an inflationary bias to government policy through the subsequent four decades. The exhaustion of technical and market possibilities for the interrelated technologies that made America the envy of the world in the 1920s contributed to inflationary private investment in the 1960s through the early 1970s. I will now digress for a while to consider how much our present problems can be attributed to some grand cycle, and how much such an attribution leaves us helpless to improve our lot.

The name that is inextricably linked to the idea of economic fluctuations that recur over intervals of half a century is that of Nicolai Kondratieff. In Moscow, during the 1920s, he was director of something called the Business Research Institute and a professor at the Agricultural Academy. He is part of the illustri-

111

ous roster of poets and scientists who created and inquired freely and disputatiously in that euphoric decade after the Russian Revolution. Early in 1930, as the capitalist world was sliding into a depression that conformed with his theories, Kondratieff was arrested and exiled to Siberia. Nothing is known about him since that time. Thus, his name is also near the top of the long, grim list of those who lost their freedom or their lives in the grasp of Stalinism. It is because of his fate, as well as his precocious devotion to mathematical statistics that Kondratieff's name has adhered to the cycle he studied. He was not its first or its sole discoverer.

Kondratieff was convinced that he had discovered a self-perpetuating cycle of prosperity and depression in the economic history of capitalist countries. If, as Kondratieff believed, it was true that each winter of capitalism prepared the ground for a subsequent spring, this could be interpreted as denying the doctrine of Marx and Lenin that capitalism was embarked on a descending course of worsening crises, the worst and last of which would terminate its existence. However, it seems much more reasonable that his downfall was due to his actual or suspected opposition to the regime, as stated by the authorities at the time.

One thing about Kondratieff's cycles was established early by his Russian critics. The rising and falling segments of these long waves could be observed definitively only in series of what economists call *nominal* quantities — money and banking statistics, lending, borrowing, and prices — rather than in series of such antonymously *real* quantities as unemployment, population, capital formation, and national production. We have already examined (in Parts I and II) a number of reasons why inflations or deflations tend to persist for more than a few years. And, at least in the case of inflations, we have looked at some reasons why they do not persist indefinitely. Kondratieff's statistics did not extend back much before 1790. They obviously could not extend forward any further than the 1920s, when he was writing. Over this 130-year interval, the waves of prices showed a rough regularity. Rising and falling prices were international phenomena, although the timing of turning points might differ by a few years among countries. Price peaks occurred around 1815, 1873, and 1920, separated by 58 and 47 years respectively. Price troughs appeared in about 1850 and 1896, a distance of 46 years. The next trough came around 1933, a distance of 37 years.

Although there are no continuous waves in the real series, there are a number of real phenomena that bear systematic relationships to the Kondratieff waves. Most major wars occur during the intervals of rising prices. Banking panics, stock market crashes, and depressions usually occupy the declining face of the wave.

Any series of economic statistics is bound to fluctuate over time. Accordingly, there will be alternating intervals of more and less growth or prosperity. Prices will sometimes go up and sometimes down. If something can be measured, and if we compute its average value over time, then it is likely to alternate between above-average and below-average values. When does such a sequence deserve to be called a cycle? Few if any semantic questions are capable of arousing so much passion among economists. While the profession is happy to acknowledge that there is a business cycle that recurs every two to ten years, there is often intense disapproval of attaching the cyclical label to sequences that recur every twenty or sixty years.

A sequence ought to be called cyclical if its recurrence is the result of some external force, as the sequence of the seasons is caused by the earth's orbit around the sun. It is equally appropriate to describe a sequence as cyclical if the momentum and position of each segment of events produces the next, as with the movements of a pendulum. If a sequence exhibits a precise tempo, like the seasons or a pendulum, it is almost certainly cyclical in one or both of these senses. However, there are cycles, such as the repeated sequence of human life from birth to reproduction to death, that can and do exhibit wide temporal variations within the broad limits imposed by human biology or another cyclical force.

The business cycle of common parlance, which is measured by the National Bureau of Economic Research and dutifully reported to be rising or falling in the newspapers, has had an average length from trough to trough of just over four years. However, just in the past two decades, we have experienced cycles as short as one year (1980 – 1981) and as long as nine years (1961 – 1970). The duration of cycles reconstructed by the National Bureau for the years 1854 – 1960 exhibits the same broad range.

At the peaks of these cycles, at least since 1920, two categories of spending have swelled to an unusual proportion of the total: business investment in inventories and consumer purchases of such durable goods as automobiles or stereos. The same two categories have accounted for a disproportionate amount of each cyclical decline in spending. The rise and fall in other categories can be accounted for by the effect on demand of the incomes generated by production of inventories and consumer durables.

Most businesses aim to keep inventories on hand that are an adequate fraction of current or expected sales of each product so that customers receive acceptably fast and efficient service. If sales are growing, for whatever reasons, then businesses also find it desirable to increase inventories. The income generated by this additional demand contributes to the growth of sales, reinforcing the rising portion of an inventory cycle. But if sales level off, even at a very high plateau, businesses merely replace inventory as it is sold, thus maintaining inventories at the desired level. The portion of production that had been devoted to expanding inventories then ceases. Incomes earned from this production also cease, causing sales to decline. Businesses then might stop purchasing even replacements for inventory that is sold, in order to reduce inventories to the lower level of sales.

By itself the inventory cycle doesn't amount to much. Since most businesses maintain small inventories relative to sales, the rate at which inventories are growing or declining has been around one percent of total income and production since the buying panic and subsequent inventory replenishment touched off by the beginning of the Korean War. As transportation has become swifter and information more plentiful, accurate, and timely, the size of inventories and the significance of their fluctuations have been decreasing steadily for over one hundred years. Because inventories are small relative to sales, they can be adjusted up or down quickly in response to fluctuations in sales. Consequently, inventory change is more a transmitter of cyclical disturbances than a primary source.

Consumer durables are another matter. Since the flowering of the auto age after World War I, they have accounted for between 7 percent and 9 percent of GNP. Cars and other consumer durables generate income and employment when they are produced and sold. It does not matter if the sale is made for cash previously saved or for money newly borrowed. However, once purchased, a station wagon, television set, or refrigerator will continue to provide useful services to the owner for many years.

We purchase our groceries almost as continuously as we eat them. These purchases are largely independent of whether or not a spouse or teen-age child can find a job, or indeed whether or not the chief income earner gets a raise or even keeps his or her job. On the other hand, although a car may be used as frequently as we dine, still, the decision to replace it with a new car will be influenced by who has a job, how much it pays, the level of interest rates or stock prices, and many other circumstances. Like decisions to increase or diminish inventories, decisions to purchase new durables or keep old ones tend to magnify good times and bad. But in that case, sales of autos and washing machines, like fluctuations in inventory investment, are only the unfolding of cycles, not the causes.

If durable goods all broke down or became too troublesome to repair after a given average amount of time — say, four years — then there would be a possibility of a self-perpetuating cycle. Any initial bunching of purchases would be followed by similar concentrations of replacement purchases at four-year intervals. A period of subnormal sales would also be echoed in the future by quadrennial dearths of business. To some extent the business cycle is governed by these replacement cycles. However, it is clear that most durable household goods do not suddenly melt after four years and do not even resemble each other in durability from one category to another. A family that trades its car in every four years can readily be persuaded to trade up after three years as a result of economic good fortune. Similarly, the same family might easily decide to keep its car for eight years as a response to adversity.

It is not surprising that neither inventory swings nor fluctuations in consumer durable purchases provide much reason for a cycle with regular timing or even very great amplitude. As noted above, the length of the ordinary business cycle has been extremely irregular. In Part I, I had occasion to observe that the peaks and valleys of the cycle were hardly visible, at least for over 25 years after the end of World War II.

A number of external forces, from natural events to wars, have been cited as explanations for the varying length and intensity of business cycles. One intriguing external mechanism, which in the American case does have a precise and appropriate periodicity, is the quadrennial presidential election, generating the "political business cycle." Of the thirty business-cycle peaks since 1854, half have been coincident with the time of presidential elections or within the subsequent year. On average, these fifteen cyclical peaks occurred just five months after election day.

A completely different cycle of roughly ten years' duration was proposed in the nineteenth century by Clement Juglar of France. Trained as a physician, Juglar left medicine in 1848, at age 29, to begin his investigations of economics. Perhaps as a result of this background, he was much more inclined to empirical research and inductive conclusions than to the rather abstract deductive reasoning that was popular among economists then as it is now. In his book *Commercial Crises and Their Periodic Recurrence in France, in England, and in America,* published in French in 1862, Juglar assembled a mass of statistics to demonstrate that the crises of capitalism took place with a more or less predictable frequency of about ten years. Juglar also argued that these crises marked similar points in a well-ordered sequence of stages that constituted a cycle. He expressed his conviction that each stage was the cause of the next in the aphorism at the head of this chapter.

Subsequent to the publication of Juglar's book, economic history gave powerful confirmation to the decadal cycle that he had discovered and to which his name was attached. In the United States, particularly serious crises marked the inauguration or early stages of business contractions in 1873, 1883, and 1893. Thereafter, the crests of less violent fluctuations occurred in 1903, 1913, and 1923. Although this nearly perfect record then broke down, an important cyclical peak was recorded in 1953, and 1973 was a major top. (Of course, half the years ending in "3" follow presidential elections, while the other half follow midterm congressional elections.)

The Juglar cycle exhibits pronounced vicissitudes of business spending on durable equipment, analogous to the fluctuations in spending on inventories and consumer durables that accompany its shorter counterpart. Business demand for machinery is similar to its demand for inventories, in the sense that both are proportionate to actual and prospective volumes of activity. An increase in volume that is perceived to be lasting will generate an increase in the purchase of productive machines. A constant level of sales will cause businesses to limit equipment purchases to the amount necessary to replace worn-out machines. A decline in activity will cause machinery orders to disappear until enough machines have worn out to reduce capacity to the desired level.

While a normal level of inventories would disappear in a matter of months, even at depressed levels of economic activity, it would take many decades before all of the boxcars, printing presses, and computers owned by American businesses were either worn out or technically obsolete. A large portion of business equipment is much more durable than any portion of the stock of household equipment. Generating plants and airplanes last significantly longer than television sets or automobiles. Thus, the echo effect on future replacement demand from any unevenness in the timing of business capital spending is considerably longer than the corresponding space between peaks and troughs in replacement of consumer durables.

Spending on productive equipment generates new incomes that increase demand for the goods produced by machines and therefore for the machines themselves. Like the shorter inventory and consumer durable cycle, the equipment cycle reinforces itself going up and down. Finally, the reduced intensity and regularity of the Juglar cycle in the twentieth century is consistent with the reduced importance of the production of goods by machines compared with intangible services and household durables.

All of this still does not explain why the length of the business equipment cycle is, or was, ten years. All we can say with confidence is that any cycle that does exist should be longer than a cycle in inventories and consumer durable goods. An additional consideration adds to this confidence. Because productive capacity is long-lived and expensive relative to inventories or family washing machines, businesses will wait longer before ordering more of it, in order to be certain that an increased level of production is sustainable. Financing must then be arranged for the new machinery. After it is ordered, machinery often takes time to produce. Thereafter it must be properly housed and brought to efficient levels of utilization. These factors also tend to lengthen the cycle of business spending on equipment. The lengthy period of high or low spending on new equipment prolongs the income effects on demand for the products of that equipment. In this way, the capital spending cycle is further extended.

Let us look at one more recognized regularity in economic activity before returning to the Kondratieff supercycle. The historical records of most industrial countries exhibit unusually regular undulations in the construction of new houses. The length of a full cycle is about twenty years. For example, in the United States peaks occurred in residential construction in the late 1880s, around 1905, the middle 1920s, the early 1950s, and, finally, twin peaks in the early and late 1970s. These cycles in the construction of new houses and apartments must be caused entirely by variations in the net new demand, since very few dwellings wear out and require replacement in periods as short as twenty or even forty and sixty years.

Simon Kuznets, one of the great economists of this or any other century, first perceived this regular movement. He then went on to describe and measure it and outline an explanation. No other person deserves such an enormous share of the credit for the knowledge that we have about the size of national income in many countries, its major components, its history, and our techniques for continuing to measure it. Kuznets has made equally significant contributions to our understanding of the division of income between rich and poor, the process of economic development, the critical economic importance of knowledge and education, and the relationship between demographics and economics.

It was in the last interaction, between population and economic activity, that Kuznets found the forces that generated and regenerated the twenty-year fluctuations. Kuznets himself began by calling these movements trend cycles, to capture the sense of a secular trend encompassing a number of shorter cycles. It is an idiosyncrasy of many economists that they cannot abide the word *cycle* applied to economic sequences with frequencies as great as twenty or fifty years. Kuznets — the recipient in 1971 of one of the first Nobel prizes in economics — retreated to calling the phenomenon he had discovered and studied a long swing.

It is now properly called a Kuznets cycle. The pendulum that governs the timing of Kuznets cycles is more reliable than the episodic excesses of caution and optimism that drive the inventory cycle or the presumed replacement cycles for appliances and machinery. The pendulum of population depends on the reality that there are minimum and maximum amounts of time after the birth of an infant before it grows old enough itself to reproduce. When people are old enough to enter the labor force and have children, they also form new households and require new homes. Fluctuations in births are echoed in the future more certainly than fluctuations in the purchase of new refrigerators or cash registers.

The baby boom after World War II was the origin of rapid growth in the labor force and new households from the mid-1960s through the late 1970s. The intervening dearth of children reflected a similar trough in births during the Great Depression. The 1980s are again a time when the population of new workers, homeowners, and potential parents is growing slowly. As mentioned already, only the boundaries of demographic behavior are predetermined from biology and past population history. The rest is a matter of human choices about whether and when to get married or establish an independent residence, whether to have children, and if so, how many. These choices are influenced by economic circumstances, changing social mores, and the disruptions of wars and other cataclysms.

The popularity of rearing children has declined with almost steady persistence since the beginning of industrialization in the United States and other developed countries. Marriages are fewer and occur later in life, and the children they produce are fewer. One effect has been to dampen the amplitude and increase the length of the population cycle. However, the economic effects are less obvious. If fewer adults are married, then a given number of them will form more separate households, occupying separate dwelling units that must be built, furnished, and serviced. Also, if fewer women and men are the parents of children, more of them can, and typically will, seek employment outside their homes.

On balance, if people form families that have children, the level of economic demand is likely to be higher and the number of job seekers lower. The economy influences these demographic decisions just as they, in turn, affect the economy, at least to the extent of accelerating or temporarily reversing the long-term trend toward a nation of unmarried adults without children. The economist Richard Easterlin, one of the most insightful of Simon Kuznets's many accomplished students, has pointed out that if young adults find it easy to obtain employment and good pay compared to the situation faced before by their parents, this encourages earlier marriages and more children.

The scarce and well-educated entrants to the labor force in the late 1950s and early 1960s found just such a favorable environment compared to the one that had confronted their parents. The resulting increase in marriages at earlier ages and with more children offset most of the depressing force of the declining Kuznets cycle after the 1950 peak. The importance of these effects is more than just the construction of dwellings, which alone accounts for between 3 percent and 6 percent of GNP. The formation of new households with children means increased demands for roads, schools, fire engines, shopping centers, furniture, appliances, and much more; not to mention the garbage collectors, policemen, schoolteachers and books, firemen, retail clerks, servicemen, electricity, and other flows of goods and labor needed to operate all of these new investments. If we add up all of the durable goods in which individuals, businesses, and governments invest as a result of population-sensitive residential construction, the total is more like 10 percent to 15 percent of GNP, or over half of all investment in durable goods. If spending on education were also classified under investment, where it belongs, both proportions would be considerably higher.

In the early 1980s, we are once again in the declining phase of a Kuznets cycle. After increasing by 22.5 percent between 1970 and 1980, the number of persons between 18 and 24 years old will decrease by about 15 percent in this decade. As a result, the potential growth of households and the labor force has been cut in half. More ominously, today's young adults look for work in the most difficult job market since the 1930s. Even when a job is available to a new worker, the real pay, adjusted for taxes and inflation, is often less than was available to the previous generation 25 years ago. Unless we take action to reverse these unfavorable trends, we face continued low demand, high unemployment, and an accelerated drift away from the reproduction of life itself.

12

The Pit

The logical expectation from the fundamental idea
would be irregularity; for why innovations which differ
so much in period of gestation and in the time it takes
to absorb them into the system should always produce
cycles respectively of somewhat less than sixty years,
somewhat less than ten years, and somewhat less than
forty months, is indeed difficult to see.

JOSEPH A. SCHUMPETER
Business Cycles (1939)

Thus far, I have examined shorter cycles whose existence is
more widely recognized and whose causes are somewhat understood, in order to lay a foundation for considering the fifty-
or sixty-year Kondratieff cycle. For the very existence of the
latter is widely disputed and its causes little understood.

A few lessons should be drawn from the preceding chapter,
before we go on. For each of the cycles considered, the volatile
elements are items that are durable in the sense that they are
expected to provide a stream of services or satisfactions over a
prolonged future: consumer durables, business inventories and
machinery, houses, shopping centers, and highways. As noted
in chapter 2, these are precisely the items that are frequently
paid for with borrowed money. The present analysis of *cycles* in
economic activity is thus in conformity with our earlier explanation of the determination of the *level* of output. If the amount
of spending on durables exerts a powerful influence on the level
of GNP, it is natural enough that fluctuations in the former
exert an equally powerful effect on fluctuations in the latter.

The proportion of production devoted to such durable goods
is the best thermometer we have to determine the cyclical tem-
perature of the economy. Readings near the upper or lower

ranges of historic experience are among the most reliable predictors of imminent reversals in the direction of employment and income. If these cycles are driven by the rise and fall of spending that is financed with borrowing, it follows that borrowing itself will swell and shrink with the development of various cycles. Moreover, as total spending presses closer to various capacity constraints and then recedes, inflation will also follow the course of the different cycles with a lag and intensity that varies with particular circumstances. (See chapter 2 and the Appendix.)

For example, in the case of the Kuznets cycle, the incomes of young couples with children tend to be relatively low while needs are high and positive expectations exist for future increases in wealth and earnings. Therefore, young adults tend to spend more than all of their incomes by going into debt. Consequently, the expanded number of new young adults from the mid-1960s through the late 1970s is another important explanation for the high rates of borrowing and inflation that characterized those years.

Price effects induced by the shorter cycles are mere ripples on the surface of the long waves in prices that were discovered by Kondratieff. Understandably, Kondratieff looked for the same underlying cause beneath the waves as the ripples. Of the many ideas that he considered and that have been elaborated by his numerous intellectual descendants, only three need concern us here.

The first involves a kind of dialectical cycle of attitudes, about which I have already commented. The experience of depression and unemployment encourages public and private behavior that breeds inflation, while the experience of inflation encourages behavior that again yields deflation and depression. The emergence over the past decade of a public policy that both tolerates and deliberately induces more unemployment as a remedy for inflation is the extant example of this phenomenon. By this reasoning, the observed periodicity of Kondratieff cycles is attributed to decision makers who are two generations removed from the most recent experience of inflation or depression.

The second line of analysis looks to a category of investment that is not prominent among the explanations for any of the shorter cycles. The long periods of time required to develop many major new sources of raw materials, especially such critical resources as food and fuel, suggest a promising possibility. Cotton from America in the early 1800s, or wheat from the Argentine fifty years later, or petroleum from the Persian Gulf fifty years after that were all vital to the continued growth of urban and industrial centers; and all required prolonged global development of the capacity to produce, transport, process, and utilize the new resources. In this view, the inflation of the Kondratieff upswing is compounded of the effects of high food and fuel prices on all other prices and the effects of sustained high investment in facilities to produce more food and fuel. When the complex chain of investments has been sufficiently completed, food or fuel prices stop rising, investment also becomes less intense, and a declining phase of the Kondratieff begins.

The third approach to explaining Kondratieffs is similar to the second, except that it focuses on the sequence of methods employed rather than the recurrence of solutions to repeated and similar food and fuel problems. Joseph Schumpeter, the great Austrian economist who spent the last decades of his career at Harvard, suggested that the innovations that decisively advanced capitalist economies occurred in great clusters. The complete evolution of each cluster required many years during which investment and price inflation were high. Thereafter, the innovations bore fruit in the form of increased goods while inflation and investment abated for a comparably long interval.

When compared to the historical evidence, each of these three explanations has some merit and some failings. For example, it is clear that the deflationary sequences that began in the 1870s and in the 1920s were characterized by conservative attitudes and public policies that were in reaction to previous experiences of explosive inflation and social turmoil. In their *Monetary History of the United States* (about which I shall say more in the next Part), Milton Friedman and Anna Schwartz present a strong case that the worldwide Great Depression was due to the actions, or more accurately the inactions, of the men who ran the Federal Reserve Bank. According to Friedman and Schwartz, these men were unable to rise above partisan, personal, and ideological concerns to meet their national and global responsibilities. When the music stopped, they did not supply the missing chairs, even though how to supply the cash demanded by depositors had been generally understood for over a century and specifically understood by the congressmen who created the Federal Reserve in 1913. The changed perspective of history made it possible for men to be blind or indifferent in 1929 to truths that had been quite apparent and urgent in 1907 or 1893.

The prototype Industrial Revolution in eighteenth-century Britain "may properly be said to have begun," according to the economic historian Nathan Rosenberg, "when techniques were successfully developed for overcoming—or, more properly, bypassing—the resource constraints which restricted the growth in industrial output of an earlier age . . . The Industrial Revolution in Britain essentially substituted cheap coal for wood as a source of fuel and power, and cheap and abundant iron for vanishing timber resources." Alternatively, the same developments can be seen as a cluster of Schumpeterian innovations: The steam engine was first used to pump water from coal mines. Coal was ultimately used to make superior iron, which was used to make the machinery in the new textile factories. Textile machines were increasingly powered by steam engines that increasingly burned coal for fuel.

Moreover, the rapid spread of these innovations in Britain corresponded with a period of rising prices. However, an almost identical set of innovations transformed America during the episode of falling prices from 1815 to 1850. Also, as Rosenberg observes, the American version of the Industrial Revolution was dependent on abundant supplies of wood for fuel and construction, many decades after the British had adopted alternative resources.

In any case, the subsequent synchronization of secular inflations with the unfolding of clustered innovations is quite unruly. The international rise in prices that begins in 1850 corresponds to a period that could be more accurately described as the maturation and deceleration of old techniques than the expansion of new ones. In contrast, and contrary to the theories just presented, the secular fall in prices from the early 1870s through the mid-1890s is accompanied by the development of modern industrial chemistry, food processing, and steel, with such dramatic manifestations as the skyscraper and the ocean liner. Finally, the matrix of tools, products, and power that defined much of twentieth-century life—electricity and oil, automobiles and airplanes, suburban houses stuffed with appliances—can be said to begin, in a rough manner of speaking, about the time of the secular price upswing from the mid-1890s. However, these related industries and activities continued to expand very rapidly right through the following price stability and decline in the 1920s and 1930s and through a good part of the next price upswing until the early 1960s.

One lesson to be drawn from this history is clear. History does not repeat itself with sufficiently precise structure or periodicity to allow us to say that if "a" happens today then "b" must also happen today or "c" tomorrow. There are, nevertheless, some generalities and congruences that might have relevance to the present. In the first place, neither deflations nor inflations last forever. In particular, the inflation that began in the 1930s was already the longest in modern industrial history as this book was being completed in 1982. However, inflations during the late Roman Empire, the high Middle Ages, and the 1500s, all lasted about a century or more. The end of an inflation has often been the occasion for, or prelude to, a particularly severe financial crisis with profound effects on real economic welfare, as in 1873 and 1929. Each of these disasters also took place during a declining period of the Kuznets population cycle, such as we are experiencing in the 1980s, with consequent weak demand for new housing, other construction, and many more goods.

There are further disturbing parallels, at least to the disaster of 1929, about which we know the most. In 1982, the wholesale prices of many basic commodities, from wheat and sugar to copper and tin, have been declining for two or three years, as was the case in 1929. Now as then, we are in the grip of conservative sentiments and conservative political leadership. In the following chapters I will examine the potential for disaster in the specific policies that have been adopted by conservative governments in the United States and elsewhere.

After World War I, the Germans were called upon to pay enormous annual sums to the British and French as reparations for war damages. Britain and France, in their turn, were obliged to pay comparably large sums to the United States as repayment for wartime assistance. Germany had no surplus of goods to export to Britain and France. Nor, therefore, did the latter two countries have any surplus to export to the United States. The system was maintained during the 1920s because the Americans lent money to the Germans, to pay the British and French, to pay the Americans, who lent it again to the Germans. The American realization that each dollar round-robin added to an accumulation of German debt that might never be repaid in exported goods brought lending to a virtual halt in the summer of 1928. The ensuing collapse of this house of cards was certainly one important cause of the international depression.

The parallel today is clear. As noted in chapter 10, most Eurocurrency loans and deposits are the result of credit extended and re-extended, first to the export customers of multinational corporations and then to the (often identical) export customers of OPEC. Difficulties involving such major debtors as Iran, Poland, Argentina, and Mexico had induced a halt to the finance of most continuing trade by the summer of 1982, threatening a further phase of violent and dangerous contraction.

It is neither instructive nor useful to interpret these similarities as a prophecy of inevitable doom. Wholesale prices declined dramatically from their 1974 peaks, with no ensuing deflation. Most declining intervals of Kuznets cycles have not coincided with depressions. As we saw in Part II, human beings can prevent any monetary system from collapsing just as surely as they created it.

With few exceptions, changes in economic tides do not result from acts of God, but from acts of men and women. We have unprecedented material and intellectual resources at hand. The entire world is within sight of vanquishing illiteracy and material deprivation. Molecular biology and physics promise the greatest advances in the history of economic progress. There is much to be done and great reward for doing it. If we are to be bound again to poverty and idleness, it will not be by fate but by our own failures of imagination and generosity.

The history of cycles, both long and short, in prices and production, is a story of economies endlessly trying to catch up with changing circumstances or to correct the excesses of previous adjustments. The existing quantity of inventories and machines is either too high or too low. The number of skilled welders seeking work is more or less than the demand. The sum of intentions to spend is greater or less than the incomes generated by current production. At present, we have an economy still geared to produce 12 million automobiles and two and a half million houses every year. It is unlikely that demand for either product will achieve such levels even briefly in the 1980s. This is partly because of demographic trends, partly because of the continuing high price of oil, partly because there are still more than 100 million serviceable automobiles in America, and partly because the car and the new suburban home have both lost some of their previous glamor.

Over twenty million workers have skills specifically developed to serve one of these two industries. Many of them are now unemployed. Two centuries ago, it took twenty-five farmers to feed every hundred men, women, and children, including the farmers. Today, we require less than two farm workers to feed the same number. Although this transition was often bumpy and painful, from today's vantage we do not view these events as the loss of 92 percent of jobs in the major area of employment, but rather as the release of those workers to enhance the achievement and diversity of our existence. We should view in the same way our reduced needs for workers making autos, houses, steel, and refrigerators. There are exciting and useful things enough to be done to keep us all busy. There are investments to be made, from public transportation to improved education, that will yield generous dividends for us, our children, and their children.

Left to its own devices, an unregulated, competitive, private economy will reach an optimum balance in the long run such that no public planner could devise a superior social outcome. Such is the unassailable teaching of classical economics. As a guide to policy, however, this doctrine is flawed by the practical handicap that effective competition is missing from large sectors of the economy. The history of cycles suggests an additional shortcoming. Changes in taste, technology, and population are always shifting the optimum balance. The economy is always correcting some imbalance in ways that lend force to Keynes's famous statement that "this *long run* is a misleading guide to current affairs. *In the long run* we are all dead. Economists set themselves too easy, too useless a task if in tempestuous seasons they can only tell us that when the storm is long past the ocean is flat again."

The economy is our ship. We are collectively its passengers, its crew, and its owners. We are entitled to steer it as best we can out of the storm's path. In the next Part, policies currently in vogue will be judged by the standard of how well they meet this mutual objective. In the final Part, I offer my own navigational advice.

PART IV

How Liberals Became Conservatives (Twice), and Why It Will Not Do to Be Either

13

Conservative Credo

To the great apostles of political freedom the word had meant freedom from coercion, freedom from the arbitrary power of other men, release from the ties which left the individual no choice but obedience to the orders of a superior to whom he was attached. The new freedom promised, however, was to be freedom from necessity, release from the compulsion of the circumstances which inevitably limit the range of choice of all of us . . .

Freedom in this sense is, of course, merely another name for power or wealth. Yet, although the promises of this new freedom were often coupled with irresponsible promises of a great increase in material wealth . . . what the promise really amounted to was that the great existing disparities in the range of choice of different people were to disappear. The demand for the new freedom was thus only another name for the old demand for an equal distribution of wealth.

FRIEDRICH A. HAYEK
The Road to Serfdom (1944)

Today, it is difficult to find an economist who still refers to himself as a Keynesian. Such are now likely to describe themselves as "neo-" or "post-" or "eclectic but mostly" Keynesian. The intent of these prefixes, simple or compound, is to apologize. Only a decade ago, conservative doctrine was characterized as neoclassical economics. Where are the neoclassical economists now that theirs is a majority view of how the world works? They have become supply side economists, believers in rational expectations, monetarists. They are unashamed to cling to the doctrinal purity of the economic theories propounded 100 years ago by Alfred Marshall and 200 years ago by Adam Smith. In this interlude of victory, they are again classicists without prefix.

133

Whatever the schisms that have divided conservative economics in the age of its renewed power, there is an area of common belief. The first credo of conservatives is that freely competitive markets, in which individuals compete to maximize their own well-being, are optimally efficient and that the real world largely comprises such markets. The asserted optimality applies not only to solving the technical problems of producing and distributing the best mix of the largest quantity of goods and services at the least cost; it applies equally to the social and ethical problems of how best to ensure justice and protect liberty.

An impressive and elegant collection of theory produced over the last two or three centuries demonstrates these optimal economic and ethical results — as long as there is indeed the perfect competition hypothesized by the theory. Assaults on the logic of this argument have been infrequent and usually unsuccessful. One notable exception was Kenneth Arrow's demonstration that neither political democracy nor marketplace democracy could be relied upon to resolve differences that were too deep or too diverse.

What divides the conservative faithful from their detractors is not so much the logic of conservative dogma as its prime postulate. Those who use the theory of competition to deduce recommendations for less social management of the economy are implicitly asserting that there is competition of the sort supposed by the theory in most of the economy, or at least that there would be in the absence of a smothering government presence. It is now generally agreed that competition is always imperfect in most markets but the conclusions of the theory of competition are left reasonably intact after allowing for some degree of imperfection. Conservatives and their opponents also agree that a profit-maximizing steel mill may rationally choose to pollute the air that all of us breathe, requiring some form of extra-market social intervention. Conservatives also concede the possibility that some things may be natural monopolies, such as turnpikes or telephones, and must therefore be regulated by society or provided by society.

But in general, those who call themselves conservatives

today are satisfied that God is in his heaven and competition permeates the world. Everyone knows that there are some monopolies, some perfectly competitive markets, and some degree of imperfection in all the markets in between. The question of whether the world we live in is or isn't competitive is therefore a question of degrees and proportions. The true believers cannot prove their faith; neither can it be disproved with mere facts. It is therefore one of those ideal issues, which abound in economics, that can be debated for centuries without definite conclusion.

Twentieth-century conservatives like to trace their ancestry directly to those who were known as liberals in the nineteenth and eighteenth centuries. For those men and women, a liberal economy, in which there would be competition without privilege, was an ideal to struggle for, not a description of reality. In economics and in politics, the liberal movement used its eloquence (and often force) to lift the restraints of feudal aristocracy and royal monopoly, to substitute reason and rules for superstition and authority. The competitive economy of Adam Smith, like the republican democracy of John Locke or Tom Paine, was a product of Enlightenment thought. It needed to be made a reality, like the Constitution or the Bill of Rights, through a continual process of attacking the vested interests and enemies of progress.

A century after *The Wealth of Nations* and the Declaration of Independence, liberal efforts had achieved great economic as well as political revolutions. With success in hand, the doctrines of laissez-faire economics attracted a new set of adherents with a new agenda. An aristocracy of industrial wealth had supplanted feudal lords. There were new powers and privileges to seek and defend. The conclusions of what had already become classical economics could be turned to defend inequality as efficaciously as they had attacked it, with only a minor shift of emphasis. For if perfect competition did in fact already prevail, then the logic of liberal economics was to leave well enough alone in the best of all possible worlds. Therefore, the distinction between the eighteenth-century economic liberal and the modern conservative is that the former fought to achieve competition while the latter defends the myth that it is already perfectly achieved.

Like the Calvinist doctrine of predestination, the belief that justice and efficiency are assured because adequate competition already exists naturally appeals most strongly to those already well favored by circumstance. Recipients of the greatest rewards from the present system are pleased to be told how optimally it solves social and economic problems and how tampering with it would be as dangerous to the commonwealth as it could be to their personal wealth. None is happier to hear the virtues of competition extolled than the monopolist; none more anxious to join the assault on granting further government privilege than the present beneficiary.

Sad to say, Adam Smith became the revered evangelist of a twentieth-century political movement that has quite properly been labeled conservative. The laissez-faire economist Friedrich Hayek, in his World War II book, *The Road to Serfdom,* entered a vigorous protest at this turn of the wheel. Disdainfully, he said in the foreword to the American edition,

> Conservatism . . . is not a social program; in its paternalistic, nationalistic, and power-adoring tendencies it is often closer to socialism than true liberalism; and with its traditionalistic, anti-intellectual, and often mystical propensities it will never, except in short periods of disillusionment, appeal to the young and all those others who believe that some changes are desirable if this world is to become a better place. A conservative movement, by its very nature, is bound to be a defender of established privilege and to lean on the power of government for the protection of privilege. The essence of the liberal position, however, is the denial of all privilege.

Who indeed would want to be labeled a conservative in the political arena of our culture, which worships youth and change, fad and fashion? Thus it happened that a new political energy appropriated the word *liberal* in the twentieth century. In some ways the new liberals could also claim the mantle of their earlier namesakes. They favored vigorous antitrust actions to thwart monopoly and gain the benefits of competition. They championed civil liberties in the tradition of Locke and Paine.

They believed a vigorous economy would solve many problems of poverty and accomplish many national objectives.

At the same time, the new liberals were part of a tendency, in the second century after Adam Smith, to compensate for shortcomings in the competitive economy on which the old liberals had so firmly relied. In the first place, perfect competition was too volatile and violent to be tolerated as a normal way of life. The emergence of corporations, labor unions, and agricultural cooperatives that were able to tame the tempests of competition was seen as the perfectly natural outcome of a process in which competition itself became an immediate obstacle to many attempting to secure wealth and income. The new liberal sought to recognize and regulate these new institutions.

More recently, liberals have recognized that even markets with large numbers of competing producers, workers, and consumers may not behave as classical theory suggests. If there is no union, cooperative, or corporation capable of controlling a market, the participants may still decide to self-impose some rigidity on the prices and relationships that characterize the market. As noted in chapter 6, this is accomplished through explicit contracts and implicit contracts that freeze prices over time and fix relationships between workers and employers, producers and consumers. This is an admirable way to enhance the efficiency of markets. However, it undermines the assurance of continual full employment and manageable inflation that can be deduced from the theory of more perfect if less efficient competition. Indeed this entirely rational and uncoerced improvement in the functioning of markets devastates the logical road from theoretical competition to social perfection just as thoroughly as does the existence of monopolistic unions and producers.

Therefore, liberal policy, even in the most advanced and earliest-developed nations, sought to preserve the benefits created by these corruptions of the ideal of perfect competition, while introducing the countervailing power of the government to mediate between or regulate powerful private institutions. If the logical conditions for the market to automatically provide full employment and stable prices were not satisfied, then it was the responsibility of government to assure the same happy outcome by intervening in the imperfect private markets.

In the last hundred years, the problem of attaining advanced industrial status has concerned much more of the world than the problem of managing it once attained. A century ago, countries like Germany, Japan, and Russia possessed many of the natural and human resources required for industrialization. The few absences stood out as barriers to progress. For example, an efficient transportation system was indispensable for advancement to the top tier of economic powers. Latecomers did not feel that they had either the luxury or the necessity to duplicate the largely unconscious, free-market means that had been employed by the first to industrialize. Where private enterprise had built most of the railroads and telegraph in Britain and the United States, the government assumed these tasks in the latecomers. The state's revenues and the state's banks often promoted industrial projects that had been privately financed in the first Industrial Revolution. Frequently the state encouraged cartels and monopolies for the sake of technical efficiency and comprehensive planning. Practitioners of the new doctrines, from Bismarck to Lenin, observed that perfect competition in the first Industrial Revolution was a cultural myth, since the leading nations had employed all of these techniques whenever they had encountered an identifiable bottleneck.

The further behind a country was at the beginning, the greater the temptations to suppress competition and substitute central power and planning. The more completely a country yielded to these temptations, the more rapidly it seemed to catch up. The new liberalism took root in the more advanced countries partly in response to the anti–laissez-faire beliefs that were dominant and often successful in the countries that were increasing their relative economic and military strength.

The modern liberal has therefore been a person who endorses the creation of artificial public rules or enterprises to make the economy more nearly like the competitive one of economic literature, or to make the consequences of a less competitive economy more nearly like those predicted in the literature, or to serve as a substitute for some prerequisites to economic growth that had emerged over centuries in the first regions to industrialize. In addition, the twentieth-century liberal is understandably skeptical of the proposition that our economy yields unimprovably just results.

In reality, the possession of wealth has meant an ability to influence private opinion and public policy. The wealthy can therefore not only affect the market through their own purchases but by influencing the spending of others (through advertising) and the government's spending of other people's money. A person with unusually large financial resources is more likely to have inherited than to have earned them. It is often difficult to perceive the positive correlation that in theory is supposed to exist between the income a person extracts from the market system and the imagination and skill with which the same person has contributed to satisfying the needs expressed in the market. Thus, the modern liberal is willing to intervene with estate taxes, regulation of campaign contributions, and minimum wages for the purpose of enforcing some standards of economic and political fairness.

For conservative defenders of the status quo against this new liberal onslaught, the orthodoxy of classical economics was an attractive bulwark. By the twentieth century the free market was no longer a standard against which its believers measured the velocity of progress, but a romantic picture of reality that was used to oppose changing it. Today, in the aftermath of sweeping victories for the second liberalism, and in an atmosphere of despair and decay, the free market has become an epic version of the golden age past. To restore it, in this view, we need only eliminate the social and economic programs of the past fifty to one hundred years.

Even after faith in the purity of free markets and their self-righting qualities became an essentially conservative dogma in the late 1800s, these ideas remained vigorous in political and intellectual life for another five or six decades. The decisive blow to conservative conviction and practice was delivered by the Great Depression or, more precisely, by the failure of the Depression to end as promptly and meekly as anticipated. This event affected the faithful like a thunderbolt hurled by a

wronged god. In putatively free and competitive markets, desperate producers and workers continually reduced the prices at
which they offered their goods and labor; and yet, goods could
not be sold nor labor employed. To all appearances, governments had done relatively little to intrude on economic activity
either before or after the Depression's onset. Where were the
technical efficiency, the moral justice, the elementary common
sense of such a hopelessly fouled system?

The faithful were routed by these events. Into the abandoned
field stepped John Maynard Keynes to expose the fallacies of
the orthodox and expound the validity of what had been her-
esy. Keynes was no more successful than those before and after
who have attempted to disprove the logic of how free markets
lead to full employment. Rather, stating that the emperor had
no clothes, he developed a theory of how economies with imperfect and limited competition could in fact generate the kinds
of permanently present and episodically severe unemployment
that in fact had characterized the history of all real capitalist
economies.

"Our criticism of the accepted classical theory of economics,"
Keynes wrote, "has consisted not so much in finding logical
flaws in its analysis as in pointing out that its tacit assumptions
are seldom or never satisfied, with the result that it cannot solve
the economic problems of the actual world." Keynes occupied
himself with observed economic behavior more than the axi-
oms from which behavior could be deduced. He argued that
wages and prices became inflexible from even a modest corro-
sion of theoretically perfect competition. Furthermore, interest
rates did not simply "clear the market" of savings supplied and
investments desired, as classical theory claimed. Interest rates
were sticky, like other prices, because of similar business conventions and habits of thought. They could not, in any case, fall
below zero. At a time when investment demand is depressed
because of high unemployment and uncertainty, individuals
might strongly prefer the safety of cash. If they sought to sell
bonds, loans, and stocks in order to raise more cash, the result
would be an increase in interest rates just when they must fall to
encourage more investment. Finally, investment is not very

sensitive to interest rates by comparison with its responsiveness to changes in employment and income. Few individuals will buy extra houses and cars just because interest rates fall. However, the jobless might make initial purchases of such items upon obtaining work. Similarly, businesses would more probably increase capacity and inventories in response to higher demand than to lower interest rates.

Keynes fashioned an explanation of unemployment and depression out of these fairly commonplace observations. If workers were unemployed, classical theory argued that their wages would fall until employers were induced to hire more workers at lower wages per person. First, this does not happen because wages and prices are inflexible. Second, even if it did happen, the decrease in wages would depress total incomes and therefore total demand. Inadequate demand could still yield unemployment. As we saw in chapter 2, demand is the key to employment, and the volatile component consisting of investment in durable goods is the key to the level of demand. But interest rates also fall slowly and incompletely in the face of unemployment, while investment is more depressed by the unemployment itself than it is stimulated by the lower interest rates. The moral is that modern states have the capacity to ensure full employment by generating a sufficient level of demand: first, by forcing interest rates lower; and second, by spending more themselves.

In the 1930s most people did not care very much whether the Depression was proof of the absence of competition or of the failure of economists' theories to comprehend the consequences of competition. What it did prove, as Keynes unnecessarily argued, was that deep and prolonged unemployment was quite possible in modern economies. The Age of Keynes was the age of commitment by governments of the industrial democracies to eliminate unemployment, using techniques that had seemed more obvious to laymen than they had to economists. For all his eloquence, acumen, and compassion, Keynes only codified trends that had been growing longer than his lifetime.

14

Conservative Practice

> Because [money] is so pervasive, when it gets out of order, it throws a monkey wrench into the operation of all the other machines. The Great Contraction is the most dramatic example but not the only one. Every other major contraction in this country has been either produced by monetary disorder or greatly exacerbated by monetary disorder. Every major inflation has been produced by monetary expansion.
>
> MILTON FRIEDMAN
> "The Role of Monetary Policy" (1968)

For a long time, the Depression loomed over economics. The hapless conservatives could not get out from under its shadow. No matter how many errors of thought they uncovered in the works of Keynes and his followers—and there were plenty of them—the plain truth for economists, plainer still for those less troubled with logical complexities, was that governments had the ability to overcome the Depression's unemployment by acting as employers of ultimate resort. The new wisdom held that free markets often didn't exist and that they were often not perfectly efficient even when they did exist.

The first serious intellectual breach of the Keynesian consensus was achieved in 1963 at the zenith of the New Economics. The critical attack was contained in the central chapter of *A Monetary History of the United States, 1867–1960,* by Milton Friedman and Anna Schwartz. Friedman had already led stunning conservative assaults on liberal fortifications, and he has led more since; but none made before or after has had such penetrating effect.

For nearly three decades, conservatives had been attacking the usurpers with little result. Elegantly but vainly, they promoted the virtues of freedom in economic and political life. A number of theoretically impeccable dissections were performed on the structure of Keynesian thought. These were accorded due respect in graduate economics courses but had little impact on political economy. The essential weakness of the conservative opposition was its failure to offer an explanation of the Great Depression that was consistent with unqualified faith in the existence and efficacy of competitive markets.

This defect was remedied by Friedman and Schwartz. Parts of their analysis have already been presented in chapters 10 and 12. They argued that the length and depth of the Depression were not natural outcomes of free market behavior but a direct result of the perverse misbehavior of the Federal Reserve System. The nation's central bank, created by the federal government for the purpose of overriding perceived defects in a competitive private bank market, had instead compounded those defects to a calamitous degree. Hence, blame for the Depression was put on meddlers with the competitive market rather than on the market itself.

If such a thesis could be supported, laissez faire would be entitled again to grace and there would be a basis for the restoration of conservative rule. Friedman and Schwartz had constructed the platform from which other conservative ideas could be broadcast. The necessity of the platform was appreciated by the conservative faithful, all of whom promptly stood upon it, and all of whom continue to pay their respects to monetarism.

Being a conservative denomination, monetarism naturally rests on the fundamental credo: Left to its own devices, a competitive market will provide optimal solutions to the problems of achieving full employment, deciding what to produce, producing it at least cost, and balancing investment for the future against consumption for the present. Further, if only it were left alone, the American economy would be just such a marvelous social contrivance.

Of course, as we have already seen, money is essential to enable any economy to achieve advanced levels of diversity, specialization, and abundance. For some time, political institutions have had the capacity to create or erase what passes for money. The account of the growth of this capacity, in Part II of this book, draws frequently on monetarist scholarship.

The distinguishing assertion of monetarism, as noted in chapter 1, is that the abuse of the capacity to regulate money has been the source of most economic evil. In the monetarist view, there is a direct proportion between the quantity of money and the total value of economic activity, much like the inescapable relation between force and velocity in physics. In particular, if the quantity of money is excessively increased, there will be an excessive increase in the value of GNP. As the increased money is supplied to an economy that is already at the perfection of competitive full employment, the total increment in value will be through inflationary price increases, since it is not possible to induce further additions to employment and production. (An ancillary tenet of conservative thought is that most of the unemployment of the past decade has not been a legitimate cause for public inducements to production. According to conservatives, unemployment has been either illusory, reflecting the mismeasurement of unemployment and the failure to adjust for the higher "normal" rates of joblessness among the increased proportion of women and teen-agers in the labor force; or temporary, as with the dislocations caused by the OPEC shocks; or frictional, as people take time to find the best job; or a result of hamstrung competition, as from labor unions or the minimum wage.)

Since the real economy will take care of itself in finding full employment and an optimum growth rate, monetarists believe that monetary policy should provide just enough money to facilitate this happy outcome. Too much money will flood the incredible engine with inflation. Too little will cause it to choke and sputter in recession or to stall into a deflationary depression.

As I have argued in chapter 1 and the Appendix, the monetarist hypothesis is a good deal flashier than the evidence warrants. In their 1963 book, Friedman and Schwartz demonstrated a general tendency for the supply of money to fluctuate in the same direction as the dollar value of economic activity and for the monetary movements to occur before the changes in output and prices. However, as already noted, the relationship has been imprecise and variable. The division of movements (allegedly caused by money) between prices and output has been uncertain and mostly in output. Every reader of the daily press knows that the definition of those liquid stores of value and potential means of payment that ought to be called "money" is a source of great confusion and controversy, as it has been for many centuries.

Nevertheless, during the past twenty years, liberals have come to admit that money does matter in our economy. Monetary policy, as Keynes himself insisted, certainly can abet or abate depression or inflation. A compromise interpretation of the Great Depression has emerged in academic circles, since the publication of the Friedman and Schwartz analysis. The initial sharp decline from 1929 to 1931 was caused by an unusual confluence of the ill winds that are always breezing about in our economy. That is to say, the capital spending cycles, inventory cycles, Kuznets cycles, and international financing problems that have been discussed already. Neither unwarranted changes in money nor other types of inept government meddling played a significant part. However, the further collapse from 1931 to 1933 was largely attributable to the failure of the Federal Reserve to perform the basic function for which it was created, by satisfying the demands of depositors (and their banks) for cash, which it had the power to create and to exchange for the overwhelmingly sound assets owned by private banks.

While monetarism has made modest progress among academic economists on the strength of modestly appealing arguments and evidence, it has achieved overwhelming dominance in the realm of public policy on a record of repeated failures. In the words of John Kenneth Galbraith, "No other course of action in economics has ever rivaled monetary policy in its capacity to survive failure." Obviously, the source of its appeal must be elsewhere. Monetarism enables conservatives to escape the Depression bogy. The recent rise of monetarism is thus in part consequent on the rise of conservatives, who must in turn continue to stand on their monetarist platform. As we shall see in a moment, there are also more venal reasons for the devotion of conservative interests to their monetarist beauty.

Why doesn't monetarism work? Or better yet, how does it work? When the Federal Reserve, or any central bank, endeavors to reduce the growth of money, it uses a handful of standard techniques. It can sell securities it owns (U.S. government bonds and bills) for money that then "disappears" from the private economy. It can be more parsimonious about money it lends to banks, or it can charge more interest for such loans. If it wants to move more forcefully, it can alter for member banks the maximum permissible ratio of their deposits to their reserves. Finally, with presidential authorization, it can move precipitously by directly regulating the quantity of new loans made by banks, through which banks create money (i.e., the 1980 credit controls).

It doesn't take a Ph.D. in economics to see that the common effect of these techniques is to make it more difficult and more expensive for individuals and businesses to borrow money from banks. As we have seen, borrowing is usually for the purpose of financing a purchase that is expensive and durable, and that is therefore expected to provide production or satisfaction over an extended future during which the debt will be repaid. If the central bank makes money more scarce and expensive—which used to be euphemistically called a "sound" monetary policy—this will clearly benefit those who already have the most money. Rarely in the history of ideas has such a transparent truth been so effectively and continuously obscured.

When money is tight, the impecunious individual, the less profitable business, and the new entrepreneur may all have to postpone their investment plans. Meanwhile, individuals with cash on hand and the strongest corporations, with established bank lines of credit or easy acceptance for their new bonds and stocks, find it relatively easy to proceed. Thus, during the monetary convulsion of 1974–75, General Motors was able to continue the enormous investments necessary to produce smaller, less polluting, more fuel-efficient cars, while Ford and Chrysler were forced to curtail their plans. The consequences are now obvious. To the extent that conservatism automatically attracts the support of those with the most to lose, the interests of its constituents are well served by a reliance on monetarism to combat inflation.

Restrictive monetary policies will reduce the growth of the quantity of money as an incidental side effect. Since the primary mechanism for the creation of new money is the creation of deposits by banks when they make loans to their customers, the growth of money will be limited in exact proportion to the limitation that higher interest rates or reserve requirements impose on the ability of customers to borrow. A monetary attack on inflation is thus actually a Keynesian attack. It "works" essentially by a reduction of total demand accomplished through a reduction of total borrowing.

After these scant observations on the workings of monetarism we are quite ready to perceive the flaw embedded in its shibboleth that the central bank controls the supply of money. In conformity with monetarist thought, almost all students are taught that the Federal Reserve can directly expand or contract the currency and deposit reserves that it supplies to the economy and thus determine the total supply of money. This proposition is correct from a legal or an algebraic point of view; but it is a woeful guide to policy. When the Federal Reserve actively pursues a course of monetary policy through any of the weapons at its command, what it actually does affects the ability of banks to lend and customers to borrow, or the interest rate at which borrowing and lending can take place. When the Federal Reserve increases interest rates it reduces the demand for loans.

Putting a true leash on supply is a far more inconceivable option. If the depositors at the First National Bank of Anytown decide that they want to hold dollar bills instead of bank deposits, it is the responsibility of the Federal Reserve to make the dollar bills available. It will convert into currency the deposits that the First of Anytown has at the Federal Reserve. Then it will lend the Anytown bank additional currency against the collateral of loans made and securities purchased by Anytown with its depositors' money. This is precisely what was *not* done during the chaotic slide into the depths of the Great Depression. That mistake is not likely to be repeated.

At the opposite end of the economic spectrum, great multinational corporations, like IBM, hold enormous Eurodollar deposits in banks outside the United States (see chapter 10). The Federal Reserve does not count Eurodollars in the money whose supply it is trying to control. Suppose that IBM decides to move $10 million from Chase Manhattan in London to Chase Manhattan in New York. This appears to have been a frequent enough occurrence in the late 1970s when the American economy grew faster than many others and multinational corporations found relatively more uses for money in the United States. As far as IBM and Chase Manhattan are concerned, one account is debited and another credited for the same $10 million. However, as far as the Federal Reserve is concerned, a net $10 million is added to U.S. bank deposits and thus to the money supply. Under the rules of the system, a new deposit must be secured by new reserves. Only the Federal Reserve can create the assets necessary to support the new deposit. If it fails to do so, it may provoke a crisis by constructing a situation in which its own rules are not satisfied, thus forcing a sudden liquidation of bank credits, a loss of confidence in banks, or both.

Thus, one way or another, the Federal Reserve supplies the cash and reserves necessary to support fully whatever liquidity has already been created. It doesn't matter if the claim on dollars was created years ago or yesterday, in Kansas or Frankfurt. These claims are so extensively fungible that the integrity of all depends on the integrity of each. The failure to maintain this integrity was the cardinal sin committed by the Federal Reserve in the Great Depression. Monetarism is built on the exposure of this transgression. Hence, its obvious paradox. A central bank that is true to its primary responsibility cannot control the supply of money. Rather, it can influence the demand for money by changing the level of interest rates.

A monetarist attack on inflation is therefore an attack on borrowing and the spending that borrowing finances. It might have been effectively used against the inflation caused by excessive corporate borrowing and investing from the mid-1960s through the early 1970s (chapter 4). However, when inflation has acquired its own momentum or is caused by a jump in the price of oil, the monetarist approach is more dangerous to the patient than to the disease. Any policy that restricts demand—whether through higher interest rates, higher taxes, or reduced government spending—will have its greatest and earliest impact on production and employment rather than on prices, as we have seen in chapter 6. If high interest rates discourage investment, the first effect will obviously be that a number of cars and houses, factories and machines, that would have been built, won't be.

Since price levels and inflation rates are quite stubborn, this phlebotomy will have to be administered for some time before inflation wanes. During this interim, higher interest rates will make a perceptible contribution to increasing the cost of everything from houses to asparagus and thus, perversely, to increasing the rate of inflation. For a considerable time, higher unemployment and lower production also will add to inflation. If General Motors makes fewer Chevrolets, it can lay off production workers and some supervisors more or less in proportion to its reduced output, but it will still have the same complement of executives and their secretaries, marketing managers, and laboratory researchers; the same interest on its debt; the same property taxes; the same rent; the same pensions for employees already retired; and so on. Therefore, many fixed costs will be spread over fewer units. Again, the initial impact of an application of monetarist restraint is to sustain inflation rather than subdue it.

Judging by recent experience, as well as by the logic of things, this opening phase—when restrictive monetary policies do all of their damage to employment and prosperity rather than to inflation—lasts about two years. Orthodox monetarism was made official American policy in early October 1979, when Jimmy Carter was still President. After monetarism became official American policy, there was an immediate jump in all interest rates. Indeed, interest rates on bonds and mortgages continued to work higher for the first two years of monetarism, and had not fallen back to the very high levels of early October 1979 when the monetarist bloodletting was halted in October 1982, one day short of its third anniversary. This is not surprising, since we have seen that the essential meaning of monetarism is nothing but high interest rates. However, this behavior was exactly contrary to the monetarist fiction that a policy of controlling the money supply would lead promptly to lower interest rates as markets anticipated lower inflation.

Higher interest rates did curtail borrowing and spending. Consequently, monetarism succeeded in raising the unemployment rate almost as promptly and sharply as interest rates. In September 1979, the unemployment rate was 5.8 percent, very close to the rate in each of the previous 18 months. The rise in unemployment provoked by monetarism was immediate and subject to only infrequent and slight reversals. In October 1979, unemployment was 6 percent. A year later, 7.5 percent of the workforce was unemployed. By October 1981, this measure reached 8 percent, and in October 1982, 10.4 percent. For more than two years, the reward for these sacrifices was not less inflation, but more. For the two years ending with the fourth quarter of 1979, prices as measured by the Department of Commerce for the entire economy increased at an average rate of 8.4 percent a year. In the next two years, the first two years of monetarism, prices increased at a rate of 8.7 percent.

By the way, the growth of money did decline. But as I have explained above and in Parts I and II, this was a decline in the demand for money caused by high interest rates and reduced production, not a restriction of supply caused by a mere turning of the monetary faucet, as monetarist theory suggests is possible. The two-year episode of increased inflation and decreased money growth in 1980–81 is yet another contradiction (in addition to those given in chapter 1 and the Appendix) of the monetarist proposition asserting a close, positive correlation between these two variables.

The first course of the monetarist meal thus turns out to be as foul in the eating as it appeared from a mere viewing. The experience in Britain, which elected the same masochistic solution to its economic problems with Margaret Thatcher in May 1979, has been very similar to that described in America. Although there is something to be said, by those who already have a lot of it, for making money dear, it is not at all clear if anyone benefits from a policy that inflicts severe wounds on stocks, bonds, real estate, and profits in addition to the damage done to its principal victims, the poor and the weak. That is a question I will consider at more length in the next chapter.

A reliance on monetarism is a reliance on prolonged unemployment and decreased profits eventually to beat inflation out of the economy. If the economy is depressed low enough and long enough, the inflexibility of prices and the momentum of inflation will be broken. General Motors will come to view the reduced level of Chevrolet sales as a permanent new norm rather than as a cyclical aberration. Plants will be closed or sold and debt reduced. Executive, administrative, marketing, and research staffs will be cut as well. The only way to limit such retrenchment is by charging lower prices to capture a larger share of a shrunken market. This means extracting wage and price concessions from employees and suppliers, who have the same motive to cut their wages and charges as General Motors does to reduce its car prices. This was the situation at last in the early months of 1982, as unemployment went above 9 percent, or ten million people, while monetarism passed its thirtieth month of destroying the confidence of businesses, workers, and investors in the economic future. Inflation finally broke.

Victories obtained by such methods are as difficult to keep as they are costly to reach. Monetarism sustains or increases inflation for a couple of years before bringing it to a fairly sharp drop. Such a sudden cessation is precisely the recipe for disaster that was explained in chapter 6. Many costs continue to reflect high rates of anticipated inflation—rents, labor and commodity contracts, and above all, after a prolonged application of monetarism, interest rates. With the end of inflation, revenues fall faster than costs. If everyone cuts prices and wages to gain market share or save jobs, then everyone is left with the same shares and the same job prospects. Only prices, incomes, and demand (measured in money) are lower. Businesses lose profits, reduce production, and fire employees. Borrowers default, and creditors foreclose on property that is falling in price.

It is bad enough that each of these events reinforces every other one. It is the peculiar curse of monetarism that it arranges to vent this catastrophe on an economy that is already severely weakened by high unemployment, depressed production and profits, and depleted financial resources. No wonder the blood-letting doctors rush to save their patient from the fatal effects of their cure just as the crisis point is approached. At the end of 1974 and again in the spring of 1980, policy swerved from bloodletting to transfusions. Pauline was saved for another episode's perils. And the inflation, so painfully extracted from her system, was restored.

One result of these experiments is that the doctors grow more impressed with the patient's fortitude. They are encouraged to go a bit further the next time, to see if they cannot reach that precise point where inflation is vanquished while the patient still lives. They might as well expect a dropped coin to land on the floor neither heads nor tails but on its rim.

15

The New
Economic Faith

ASSUMPTIONS IN CORPORATE BUDGETS DON'T
MESH WITH SUPPLY SIDE VIEW
Wall Street Journal, September 1981

This administration . . . has provided just what American industry said it needed to transform our economy . . . We have sounded the clarion call to economic
arms. Yet, I must stand here today and ask: Where is
the business response? . . . Where are the new plants?
Where are the expansion plans?

DONALD REGAN
Secretary of the Treasury, September 1981

And yet nothing has been changed except what is Un-
real, as if nothing had been changed at all.

WALLACE STEVENS
"As You Leave the Room" (1957)

The economy is like a human organism. If the leeches of severe
monetary restraint are applied too intently for too long, the
damage done may not be easy to reverse. Simply removing the
leeches or providing a fresh transfusion of plentiful money at
low interest rates may fail to restore the patient. Such was the
apparent condition of the American and world economies in
1982. The Federal Reserve retreated from monetarism with the
same alacrity that it had displayed in 1974 and in 1980. Interest
rates fell and the quantity of money expanded more vigorously.
In August, there was a great show of determination not to permit a Mexican debt default or the associated risk of a storm of
interrelated failures. In October there was an atypically public

renunciation of the further pursuit of monetarist policy. Democratic gains in the November elections added further plausibility to a change in the course of policy toward more concern
with growth, employment, and survival.

But the economy did not respond. Lower interest rates could
not induce the unemployed and those fearful of becoming unemployed to borrow money for the purchase of new houses or
videotape recorders. Businesses were not inclined to borrow
money for new investments when prior investments stood idle,
growth was very low, and profits were depressed. The major
lenders in the Eurocurrency game were quite properly scared.
Even while the system did not collapse, new credits were severely reduced, with a consequent reduction in worldwide exports and imports. There was a remote possibility that the patient could again be restored to his previous condition of
modest growth with modest inflation, but everyone also had to
consider the possibility that the monetarist medicine had been
applied beyond the point that produces a pandemic of fatal deflation and depression.

In the conclusion I shall propose policies appropriate to these
respective circumstances. First, in this chapter, I shall further
consider why men and women who wish their country no harm
have repeatedly prescribed such dangerous and ineffective
remedies. To do so, I shall have to examine recent political history and the sophistries and eccentricities that have bloomed in
the garden of economic doctrines.

When the Reagan administration came to power at the beginning of 1981, two quite antithetical and hostile philosophies
were simultaneously installed. They attracted support from two
equally different constellations of interests. The felicitous pen
of Herbert Stein has named them both: main-line conservatism
and supply side economics. The conservative credo is common
to both, but they share it as uncomfortably as the Jews and
Arabs do Palestine.

We have already had a look at the main-line conservatives in
chapter 13. For them, the free market is a conceptual shield for
defense of the status quo, not a utopia whose achievement defines the continuing obstacles that must be surmounted. During
the past fifty years, the Keynesian state has become an estab-

lished reality. Further, it has proved its effectiveness at maintaining high rates of economic utilization and social stability. These are good results for rich and powerful corporations and individuals. The heyday of Keynesianism was also a golden age for profits, the stock market, and the general comfort of the well-to-do. Accordingly, today's main-line conservative defends the modern welfare state as vigorously as his predecessor opposed its advent in the 1930s.

Over the decades, a complex network of accommodation developed between many powerful corporations and the state which had assumed responsibility for economic management and regulation. The largest corporations discovered that they were equipped to cope with the expensive complexities of bureaucratic regulation to the effective exclusion of new or weak competitors. Further, by a process that is now well understood, they were often able to strongly influence the regulatory process itself. In fact, as many aging industries encountered the difficulties of senility over the past two decades, they were able to call on the federal government to preserve their existence and to protect the interests of their owners. This is the only reasonable interpretation of the federal interventions for the benefit of the creditors and stockholders of Penn Central and other railroads, Lockheed, and Chrysler.

Main-line conservatives have a natural preference for implementing Keynesian management of the economy with monetary policy rather than with spending or taxing policy. As already noted, a restrictive monetary policy to combat inflation clearly enhances the relative advantage of those who have the most money or the easiest access to money. A stimulative fiscal policy is most efficient as well as equitable if taxes are imposed on the rich, who spend less than all of their incomes, while spending is diverted to the poor, who convert all of their receipts into effective demand. A stimulative monetary policy, while it may provide easier opportunities for new challengers to the establishment, also benefits the wealthy by depressing interest rates and thereby increasing the value of all categories of income-producing assets, the ownership of which is the defining feature of wealthiness.

Main-line conservatives are not notable for strict adherence to logical principles. This is not surprising, inasmuch as their staging point is the perversion of the pursuit of free markets into the proposition that the objective is already achieved. Milton Friedman had no qualms about the use of American military force to insure that the Vietnamese would choose to be free to choose. I remember an afternoon at Columbia University in 1967 when Arthur Burns berated an official from the Agency for International Development for the continued provision of American food and other aid to India at a time when that country had chosen to proceed with the development of publicly owned steel mills and fertilizer plants. Yet, so far as I know, the Chairman of the Council of Economic Advisors under President Eisenhower, Chairman of the Federal Reserve Board under President Nixon, and Ambassador to West Germany under President Reagan never advocated expelling Britain from NATO, despite that country's equally grave lapses into socialism.

Positions fall into a more comprehensible mental order if one supposes that the main-line conservatives have had a constant purpose for the past one hundred and twenty-five years of American experience. Often unconsciously or accidentally, they have gone about the truly conservative business of preserving the interests of those individuals and institutions that are already best served by our political economy. The rise and fall of doctrines ardently proclaimed among them makes sense if viewed as a succession of different techniques that are sequentially appropriate to achieve the same objective, like the series of tools employed by a dentist at work on the same cavity.

For main-line conservatives, the proper remedies for inflation have been stated by Herbert Stein, who puts himself among the main-liners: "The process of getting inflation down will probably require a transitional period of unusually high unemployment. . . Getting inflation down and then stabilizing the price level will require first reducing and then stabilizing the rate of growth of the money supply."

It is no hyperbole to state that the influence of these views in the present administration results from the power and money of

their adherents. The electoral triumph of 1980 consumed
wealth and influence on a large scale. Public-issue corporate
advertising was an important element in the decisive victory of
conservatism.

Supply side economics is a genuinely alternative approach to
the world. As their appellation suggests, supply siders reject the
focus of Keynesian analysis on the adequacy of effective demand for the goods and services that an economy can produce.
Instead, they emphasize the importance of increasing the supply of useful output that an economy is able to provide. Suppose we start with an optimally efficient, competitive economy.
Along come some stargazing Keynesians who impose various
taxes and subsidies in order to insure that the improvident are
not bereft in their retirement and, more important, that total
demand exhausts the total supply of economic activity. The
point of supply side doctrine is that these interventions will
prove self-defeating.

As the tax on incomes increases, workers, investors, and en-
trepreneurs will be less inclined to produce and create. Even if
the money that the government takes in taxes is all spent by the
government or those to whom it is given, higher tax rates will
curtail the supply of goods while the demand for them is maintained or increased. At higher tax rates, workers will be discouraged from working because their after-tax pay is reduced,
or employers will not hire so many because their cost is increased, or some combination of these effects will occur. Similarly, borrowers will pay more and lenders will receive less.
This will discourage the saving and investment that expand future supply.

More than half the expenditures of the federal government
are transfer payments to those who are retired, unemployed,
children of the unemployed, or otherwise in need. In the supply side view, this amounts to paying people for not working.
Thus, while taxes discourage workers and their employers, a
large portion of Keynesian expenditure also inhibits the supply
of productive effort.

All of this appears reasonably logical as far as it goes. However, the argument cannot be completed without considering

the value that workers, businesses, and investors place on the government goods, services, and transfers that are funded with their tax dollars. I have already argued in chapter 7 that the Social Security tax has severe effects on employment and inflation, just as the supply side analysis would suggest. However, Social Security benefits are certainly perceived as valuable by the workers who are earning them, and by employers as well, to the extent that their own liability for retirement payments is reduced. In urban locations especially, police and fire departments, water supply, public transportation, garbage collection, and similar services are more valuable to the taxpayers than any alternative private arrangements they might have made. A New York City worker who earns $80 a day and pays the city $2 or $3 for these services has clearly gotten more than his money's worth just by being able to ride to work and back for $1.50 a day on the bus or subway, rather than paying $5 to $10 a day by taxi.

The public services paid for by taxes are usually available without distinction to those who do not produce and therefore have no incomes on which taxes are paid. This creates at least a logical possibility to maintain the supply side notion that taxes progressively destroy production. If people earn enough for not working so that they can pay the subway fare, buy groceries, and furnish and rent an apartment, then they can benefit from the services provided by the taxes paid by workers. If they also find work repugnant and idleness gratifying, then truly rising tax rates could translate into declining productive effort. Thus, supply side economics rests on one or more of the following three propositions, none of which is ever stated explicitly: 1) Government goods and services are worth far less than the tax money they cost. 2) The unemployed and their dependents are too generously rewarded for their plight. 3) Most people would rather loaf than work.

We are all aware of government programs for which we pay but from which we do not benefit. Those who drive to work or take taxis may not benefit from taxes paid for public transportation. Those without children get little in direct return for their school taxes. These are classic political issues for which supply siders may urge different solutions. There may be much in favor of having the costs of subways borne entirely by riders rather than by taxpayers, and the costs of schooling paid by the parents of students rather than by the public. However, there are clear benefits to commerce and production as well as the general welfare if employers and vendors can attract workers and customers through an inexpensive transportation network. The social and economic benefits of a universally high standard of education are undeniable. There is much to be said not only for the collection of one's own garbage but for the disposal of the neighbors' garbage. Proponents of supply side theory have been at some pains to emphasize that they are not necessarily advocating the elimination of any present public programs.

Do we pay too much to the unemployed and for the support of their children? If so, we have at least one program that can be cut. There are many imperfections in the design and administration of various welfare programs and transfer payments; however, it strains credulity to argue that our society offers pay for indolence that rivals its inducement for effort. This leaves only the possibility that many people find work so disagreeable that they would suffer considerable material sacrifices to substitute the pleasures of indolence. It is curious that academic economists, from the classical right to the Marxist left, persist in making acute aversion to work a cornerstone of their theories, while they themselves exhibit an enormous appetite for their own work that is unrelated to direct or alternative financial rewards. Underground mining and rowing galleys have always been work well worth avoiding. But such tasks have been the exception in human society, not the rule. Most of us derive some pride and satisfaction from our employment. Joblessness, in contrast, produces frustrations and discontents beyond its financial consequences. We are profoundly social animals. Like beavers or ants, we are moved to contribute to our community by more than the pecuniary rewards of the market.

Supply side theory does not explain the basic facts of recent economic experience any better than it satisfies the requirements of reason. From the mid-1960s through the late 1970s, marginal tax rates did rise steadily and substantially. This was a period of deteriorating real economic growth and of expanding inflation. However, as we have already seen in Part I, the supply of capital goods grew at record-breaking speed in the first half of this interval. After the first OPEC price shock, the growth of capital supply was slower but still respectably positive by any standard. The labor force grew at historically high rates through the late 1960s and the 1970s. In part, this was for purely demographic reasons. However, contrary to supply side reasoning, the percentage of working-age people who actually sought work expanded from the average postwar level of 59 percent in the mid-1960s to a record high of 64 percent by the end of the 1970s, despite rising marginal tax rates and the increasing proportion of job seekers unable to find work.

Ideas have their own lives and vital characteristics. Often, however, no matter how sincerely disinterested their originators might be, ideas also attract mundane constituencies. The singular idea of supply side economics that has captured popular understanding and attracted a constituency is that, in theory, tax rates may be so high that total revenue will be increased by lowering them; and that this was the condition of the United States in 1980. The theory is summarized as the Laffer Curve, after the economist Arthur B. Laffer, who is said to have drawn one on a napkin in a cocktail lounge in 1974. The curve is also the entire proof of the proposition. The tax rate (as a percentage of national income) can vary only from 0 percent to 100 percent inclusive. If the tax rate is zero, then clearly the revenue of the government will also be zero. As taxes are imposed at increasing rates, government revenues will also increase by taking a larger portion of total production. However, higher tax rates will discourage the supply of labor and capital and hence shrink the GNP pie, of which the government is taking an ever-larger slice.

To see that this will eventually result in lower government revenues from higher tax rates (or vice versa), the supply siders ask you to contemplate the situation at the extreme case of a 100 percent tax rate. No one, they argue, will produce anything if all of their production is taken away. Hence, there will be nothing for the government to take; and total government revenues will once again be nothing. The Laffer Curve is thus neatly tied down to zero at both ends of the tax-rate measuring stick. Tax rates in between yield some positive revenue out of some positive production. Therefore, there must be a maximum revenue point someplace in the middle. Any tax rate higher than the one that produces this maximum revenue is going to produce the same government revenue and less national output than would be obtained from some lower tax rate on the other side of the maximum. The lower rate is obviously superior.

The fallacy in this argument is an extension of the earlier error. What would any government do with 100 percent of the national product? The supply side sermon against taxes is based on a parable at 100 percent rates of a mercilessly satanic government that takes everything and returns nothing, thus ensuring that all of its citizens promptly die whether or not they work. Only those who escape from this hell or conceal their productive activity within it will survive. Obviously, such societies cannot be observed. Perhaps the closest examples were plantations worked by slaves, with the owner equivalent to a government entitled to 100 percent of production. However, a prudent slave owner devoted some portion of total production to providing for the energy, longevity, and reproduction of his slaves. As a result, slave plantations did produce output and their owners did earn revenues. The communist economy of the Inca empire also laid claim to just about 100 percent of wealth and income without causing production to cease or eliminating the luxury and power of the emperor.

So long as governments give back at least some fraction of what they take, there is no reason why tax rates cannot be 100 percent. The right side of the Laffer Curve is not tied down to zero. Its rise or fall depends as much on what and how governments return as on what they take. There is no reason in principle why the graph of government revenues might not be a perfectly straight line that rises from nothing when taxes are nothing to 100 percent of the maximum GNP at the maximum tax rate. The Laffer Curve implicitly assumes that all of the services, goods, and transfer payments, that are or might be provided by governments, are totally worthless to the sustenance of life or spirit.

Supply side economics might have undertaken a serious political assault on the government programs that it considered most dispensable or readily subject to improved efficiency. However, all of these programs have supporters. Therefore, the popular version of supply side economics maintained (from the Laffer Curve) that we could simply cut taxes without cutting the programs that taxes paid for. The result would be such an increase in the supply of output that tax revenues would still pay for the programs at lower tax rates; the growth of private production would cause a relative decline in the government sector, and the reduction in unemployment payments and similar benefits would cause an absolute decline. Finally, under the cold water of unbottled competition, inflation itself would melt like the Wicked Witch of the West.

This fairy tale achieved a political importance out of all proportion to its plausibility. Cutting everybody's taxes is an eternal formula for universal acclaim. It was the main course of the political menu offered by Ronald Reagan and endorsed with his overwhelming victory. While main-line conservatives have influence in the Reagan administration because of the established wealth and power they represent, supply siders have influence because of the votes that they provided. The success of the almost transparent fictions of supply side economics at concealing the true effects of tax cuts from most voters and many knowledgeable people must be attributed more to the state of society than the artfulness with which a curve was drawn. Mass delusions are usually in the eyes of the beholders.

The tax revolt in the late 1970s was a taproot of the supply side frenzy. In the mid-1950s, governments at all levels extracted about $100 billion from a GNP of $400 billion, or 25 percent. Twenty-five years later, governments' take had expanded to about $1 trillion out of a GNP of $3 trillion, or 33 percent. Taxes had gone up a third more than inflation and real growth combined. But many taxpayers felt that the value of government services received in return had declined. Police pay and school budgets had risen in step with crime and functional illiteracy. Urban renewal and antipoverty programs seemed to have betrayed their titles. The federal government no longer presided over the stability and prosperity that had justified its growth. The supply side movement captured a widespread despair about the honesty, effectiveness, and morality of large institutions, especially governments. In this sense, the supply side movement was a beneficiary of Vietnam and Watergate, a descendant of the antiauthoritarianism of the antiwar movement and of the skeptical appraisal of the Keynesian bureaucracy contained in the 1972 Democratic Party platform on which George McGovern had run.

While this bitterness was widespread, it was most intense among the young. They felt the deepest disillusion at the failures of the new liberal society to reach the hopes of their parents. Theirs was the strongest economic disappointment as well. Education did not always deliver its promised rewards. Jobs were hard to find. Inflated housing prices, taxes, and mortgage rates made home ownership unobtainable for many whose parents had readily managed. Surrounded by these oppressions, young adults naturally turned to the evil that they could organize to reduce directly: taxes.

The business adherents of supply side doctrine suffered less critical frustrations. They too are often younger people. More important, their firms are often newer, smaller companies that have grown rapidly. Frequently these companies have utilized new technologies and new methods of doing business. They have offered solutions to the problems posed by the decline of traditional industries, lagging productivity, inflation, or high energy prices. They are the "high-tech" firms, the members of the recently formed American Business Council. The owners of these companies are often the new millionaires who have appeared in such abundance since the early 1970s. Their workers are usually not unionized and frequently are well educated and highly skilled. In these respects, they correspond well with the employee groups who have given the strongest support to supply side initiatives. For the latter often have above-average skills and ambitions; are frequently members of, children of, or aspirants to the middle class; and are less often union members, whose wages have stayed ahead of inflation since the 1960s.

The political thrust of such a movement follows from the hopes and frustrations of its members. They would like to clear the dead growth of a prior season to make way for the new. They are anxious to accelerate the disappearance of the giant firms that are perceived as no longer contributing to society. Thus David Stockman was the only congressman from Michigan to vote against the Chrysler rescue plan. If the Japanese make better and cheaper cars, let Chrysler's workers be released to make photovoltaic cells or home computers. The unions, which typically have organized precisely these older firms, are seen as malignant contributors to inflation and inefficiency.

Events in the last twenty years have led to a widespread perception that the public employee unions are enemies of the public, responsible for the growth of government costs and the decline of government services. For the supply side movement, the enormous government establishment itself is an enemy, first, because it has been the supportive ally of embattled old businesses and unions, and second, because of its own perceived corruption, inefficiency, and impact on inflation.

The supply side movement does not have the intellectual perspicacity of the first liberal movement, as expressed by a Benjamin Franklin, nor of the second liberal movement, as expressed by a Lord Keynes. However, it shares with them a determination to overcome its frustrations in order to achieve its vision of a better future. The dead growth on which supply side trains its wrath is the analogue of the monarchist mercantilism that attracted the scorn of Adam Smith or the classical complacency that fell before the New Deal. Supply side is, in a very real way, the one strand in the American polity that views the future with some optimism.

If the supply siders represent the third generation of liberals, however inept and narrow, then clearly the second generation must have passed into the realm of conserving rather than improving. Many who still go by the name "liberal" have become the true allies of the main-line conservatives. Both seek to defend the extent of the existing Keynesian state. Both seek to preserve the power and wealth of old industries and established unions. This is the true significance of proposals for the "Reindustrialization of America." Both are too worldly wise to believe the nostrums of supply side faith. Both would like to end inflation at someone else's expense. Both are fearful of the future and scared to rock the boat, even in the present.

The division between supply siders and main-line conservatives in the Reagan administration was thus foreshadowed in the Carter administration by the fatal conflict between those around the President, who were willing to look for the future, and those behind Senator Edward Kennedy, determined to re-create the past.

And now at last we can see more clearly why our ailing economy has been so maltreated with monetarist medicine. On one side of the present administration we have the conservatives (once- and twice-removed liberals), who are happy to use monetarism as a weapon against inflation since they view it as the least evil, least disruptive alternative. On the other side are the enthusiastic tax cutters, spending cutters, and deregulators. For these supply siders, monetarism is reluctantly endorsed as a logical concomitant of belief in the free market. In fact, many supply siders have tried to escape the discomforts of monetarism by retreating still further into the past and advocating the classical gold standard. It was easiest for the supply siders to win political approval for tax cuts, because these were most popular and least threatening even to conservative interests.

But there is another force in our drama besides the factions contending in the Congress and the White House. The men and woman who determined the policy of the Federal Reserve System in the early 1980s consisted in part of devoted believers in the divine commandment for sound money, the sort of zealots bred in the private banking and Federal Reserve systems, whose convictions run far beyond the common sense of ordinary main-line conservatives. Add to these a substantial number of main-liners who believed with George Bush that supply side tax cuts are dangerous "Voodoo Economics" and an equal number of latter-day-liberal Democrats who believed the same thing for somewhat different reasons. Remember that everybody wanted to see the supply siders get their electoral comeuppance from a punk economy in November 1982, and that the Democrats wished the same fate on all Republicans and their President. Observe that the very intended victims of this attack in the Congress and in the White House were busy encouraging their attacker with anything from nominal to sincere praise for the virtues of tight money. Note, finally, that the Federal Reserve applied repeated and increasingly severe episodes of bloodletting to the economy through the 1970s, which neither killed the patient nor cured the inflation. This only emboldened them to imagine that even more severe treatments might prove effective but still not fatal. Thus, when Ronald Reagan was inaugurated, the stage had been perfectly set for a possibly fatal monetarist assault on the economy.

PART V

Conclusions

16

Bringing Inflation Down to Earth

> When investment is planned and debts incurred on the
> basis of expectations that inflation will continue, a
> check to rising prices would cause acute financial em-
> barrassment and might precipitate a sharp slump. An
> inflationary economy is in the situation of a man hold-
> ing a tiger by the tail.
>
> JOAN ROBINSON
> *Economic Heresies* (1971)

The Reagan administration has been, from the beginning,
knocking inflation down with a crash. As we have already seen,
its encouragement of stringent monetarism pushes the economy
toward a cumulating crisis. And the supply side of the administration abjures "quick fixes"—or any other kind of fix—for
unemployment. An equal abhorrence has been expressed for
saving or shoring up failing and bankrupt firms or financial institutions. The effect of this policy is to restore the vicissitudes
and dangers of the free market.

The resulting termination of inflation is therefore identical to
the terminations of most extended inflations that were wrought
by the free market in the centuries before Keynesian policy.
Inflations were often crushed by a massive avalanche of collapsing credit and money, falling incomes, prices, and confidence.
The result was to pummel the economy and society as flat as the
inflation. If history repeats, the present chapter will be only a
postmortem. Even so, it will still be useful to the present generation in assessing blame for failed policies by comparison with
the alternatives, and, I hope, to a future generation confronted
with similar problems. My hope is that the present course of
events will evolve slowly enough to give us time to consider a
more enlightened disengagement from inflation.

169

I propose four characteristics that should be evident in any intelligent plan to end inflation. Such a plan should be 1) *realistic*, in the sense that it is capable of achieving its objective without unbearable costs; 2) *commanding of broad popular support*, without which it will not in fact be realistic; 3) *equipped with effective penalties and inducements* to obtain compliance; and 4) *believable*. A plan that satisfies the first three requirements will be believable and a plan must be believable to be realistic and to obtain wide support.

In an economy addicted to inflation, as ours was quite thoroughly by the early 1980s, a realistic plan necessarily implied a gradual and measured reduction of inflation. Otherwise it risked driving the economy into depression or lurching back into inflation. If inflation and interest rates come down slowly, there is time for debt to be refinanced, plans to be reformulated, and wage contracts to be gradually moderated without leaving the most recently adjusted unfairly ahead or the next to be adjusted unfairly behind. Above all, the rate of inflation decline must be gradual enough so that businesses with fixed wage and interest commitments do not fail and consumers with mortgage debts do not have to default. When Ronald Reagan was inaugurated the addictive rate of inflation was about 10 percent. The appropriate rate of deceleration is calculable from a rather laborious examination of detailed economic data. In my judgment, the tolerable rate of descent, as of early 1981, was no greater than 2 percent a year. In that case, a realistic plan would have anticipated price stability no earlier than the beginning of 1986. A plan to end that addictive inflation should thus have extended over a period of about five years.

A realistic plan must also see to it that prices come down at roughly comparable and coincident rates in different sectors. Otherwise, one group's lagging deceleration will become another's unaffordable costs. Product prices cannot come down faster than wages, or businesses will lose their profits and fire their workers. Farm prices cannot come down too fast, or farmers will be bankrupted; nor too slowly, or urban workers will find that their real wages are falling.

These considerations also illuminate the problem of obtaining broad support. Obviously, a program of prolonged, intricate, and difficult adjustment to stable prices will require nearly unanimous support from voters and economic decision makers. It is undesirable as well as unnecessary that a process of disinflation should affect the relative standing of regions, classes, sectors, or industries. It is self-evident that the same or an expanded real income in a world of no inflation could be divided among labor, profits, retirees, and other groups, just as it had been under inflation. Any disinflation plan that imposes disproportionate burdens on one class or sector invites a debilitating resistance. It is an additional disadvantage of monetarism that it inflicts the majority of its heavy costs on workers and businesses that produce goods typically purchased with borrowed money, such as autos, houses, and capital equipment.

An effective plan, capable of mobilizing popular support, would not and need not impose heavy burdens on any group. Inflation entails few groups of unambiguous winners or losers. Its costs are insidious, gradual, and ubiquitous. The burden of ending it should be equally diffuse.

A disinflation plan that included a continued Keynesian commitment to high employment would clearly be perceived more favorably than one which did not. One important element of truth in the supply side theology is the tenet that prosperity is consistent with disinflation. Periods of rapid economic growth and high capacity utilization have also been periods of substantial gains in productivity. At any given rate of increase in wages, a more rapid increase in output per hour implies a less rapid increase of labor costs and prices. The supply side view is also quite correct in observing that the expense of supporting those who are not productively employed must add to the costs of production through taxes or inflationary debt financing.

So far we have observed that an intelligent plan for disinflation must extend over a number of years, must preserve a rough balance among a myriad of relative wages and prices, must maintain a Keynesian commitment to high employment and rapid growth, and must attract nearly universal support and compliance. Since this is not a book about political science or sociology, I rely on the reader's common sense to see that these objectives are not obtainable in our society unless the disinflation plan is accompanied by inducements and penalties for the behavior of individuals and institutions.

Mandatory wage and price controls impose penalties for the illegal act of raising the price of anything above some specified level or rate of change. Since the experience with the Nixon controls in the early 1970s, there is now widespread belief that such an approach is harmful and doomed to failure. It is worth briefly outlining the reasons why this is a generally correct view, as well as the reasons that make controls especially inappropriate as a response to a high rate of addictive inflation.

The primary problem with controls is that there is too much to control: millions of prices in millions of locations at which there occur over a billion transactions every day. Direct enforcement would require a government apparatus unimaginably large, expensive, and oppressive. Thus, mandatory controls can work only if they are voluntarily respected. In the past, respect has been induced by patriotism, the conviction that controls would do more good than harm, and a perception that the source of the inflation was temporary and unavoidable. For all of these reasons, wage-price control programs have been particularly successful during the conduct of wars. Today, popular skepticism about controls is reason enough to forget about them.

The skepticism also has objective foundations. In many markets, the regulation of prices by government edict does more damage to the functioning of prices as signals of relative shifts in supply and demand than the similar damage done by inflation itself. This is true even in markets of very imperfect competition and infrequent price changes. Consequently, mandatory controls have usually been accompanied by cumbersome bureaucracies to adjudicate disputes and adjust relative prices. The longer controls are kept in place, the more serious are the resulting maladjustments.

Imposing controls on an economy experiencing a bulge in military expenditures has quite different prospects for success compared with imposing them on an economy that has already incorporated higher expected rates of inflation into its contracts and customs for wages and interest rates. Many long-term loans at 15 percent and 20 percent interest result in defaults if inflation is stopped suddenly. There are always a variety of labor and commodity contracts that specify periodic wage and price increases in the future, in return for which one or another party may already enjoy some present benefit or endure some temporary sacrifice. In those prevalent cases where wages and prices adjust to inflation but do so infrequently in order to preserve the advantages of fixed prices in the interims, a sudden interruption of the process will necessarily leave some unfairly and inefficiently behind and others ahead.

Under such conditions, the controllers must get into the detailed, and constitutionally questionable, business of revoking and recasting millions of explicit and implicit contracts. Even the modest temporary success of the Nixon controls in the early 1970s had become problematic by the early 1980s because of the substantially higher momentum of wages and level of interest rates. However, it should be noted that the two most important reasons for the failure of the Nixon controls were avoidable and accidental, respectively. The controls were employed to repress the effects of a deliberately inflationary monetary and fiscal policy. Their dismantling coincided with the first OPEC price shock.

"Voluntary" controls, or wage-price guidelines, avoid many of the problems of mandatory restraints by simply abstaining from many dimensions of inflation. Both the Kennedy and the Carter guidelines simplified the enforcement problem by focusing on a few thousand of the largest private firms. A further simplification—and concession to the useful roles of prices and wages as rewards and signals—specified average rates of change for wages and prices for each enterprise. Businesses, workers, unions, and customers were left free to change the relative rates of pay and prices among a business's many workers and products. Even those contracts that were subject to guideline scrutiny could always violate the standards whenever the urgency of economic pressures was stronger than the desire to avoid government displeasure and public exposure.

It is fair to say that voluntary guidelines have been less harmful precisely to the extent that they have been less effective. The moderations associated with the Kennedy guidelines in the early 1960s and the Carter program in the late 1970s lasted a few years and then vanished like startled fish.

Once an economy is adjusted to the expectation of continuing high inflation, it is ineffective or unacceptably damaging to try to compel people to transact their affairs at prices different from those they would have employed without compulsion. This principle applies equally whether the compulsion is in the form of political controls or economic distress. What is needed is a plan that disturbs properly determined relative prices even less than voluntary guidelines, while, at the same time, it changes expectations about inflation in such a way that people are persuaded to behave in conformity with the plan's broad inflation assumptions. That is, under an ideal plan, average changes in wages, prices, interest rates, and other numbers that reflect and cause inflation would just equal the planned numbers as a result of private decisions in private markets. In repeated transactions and negotiations, the outcome that is viewed as optimal will reflect the planned rate of inflation, as well as all the nuances of tenure and quality, skill and location, that go into the determination of any specific price, wage, or fee.

At the end of World War II, the government of France confronted a similar perplexity. After almost half a century of anemic economic growth, the universal expectation was for continued lagging performance. These expectations were reflected in plans—actually, the absence of plans—for investment in education, new construction, equipment, and products. In this way the expectations became self-fulfilling. Puny investment assured puny growth. The chief component in the successful response of the French government to this situation was called indicative planning. It is principally associated with the name of Jean Monnet, whose imagination did more for the postwar recovery of France and the economic integration of western Europe than the ideas or resources of any other contributor.

Ideally (and the actual implementation was far from ideal),

the indicative plans achieved their purposes through two mechanisms. First, the plan was a concrete description of a more rapidly growing and prosperous economy, which was technically feasible. This feasibility was made believable by displaying in some detail how the plan could be achieved year by year; and what the interrelated requirements would be for outputs, inputs, investments, employment, and skills in each sector. This detail also made clear that, and how, the rewards of an enlarged economy could become the enlarged rewards of every class and sector. This gave the plans their ability to command support as well as belief. For private business, in the words of Stephen S. Cohen, "The motor of indicative planning is a benign circle: the more industry follows the plan, the more accurate the plan's information will be; the more accurate the plan's information, the more reason industry will have to follow the plan."

This is probably too benign to have worked effectively by itself in postwar France or to work in present-day America. The second mechanism of indicative planning operated through the convenient fact that the French government was itself the owner of vast portions of the French economy: all the railroads, airlines, electric power systems, and large portions of banking, the automobile industry, and other sectors. By itself, the government could promise to provide its substantial share of the goods, facilities, and employment envisioned by the plan, and to purchase its share of the output called for from others. This undertaking gave the plans a much greater probability of realization.

Both of these mechanisms are available to the government of the United States to ensure that an indicative plan to end inflation would be successful. There never has been a government that knew so much about the economic resources and products of its domain. Moreover, the federal government spends an amount equal to one quarter of GNP, while its true economic muscle is enlarged further through tax and regulatory policies. A plan to end inflation would renew the Keynesian commitment of the federal government to use its fiscal and monetary power to maintain total demand at levels high enough to employ a growing labor force and expanding capital facilities. As argued above, this would both gain necessary support for the plan and make the elimination of inflation more swift and painless. In the next chapter, I will suggest how these policy instruments, especially the mix of federal spending and taxing, could be used more effectively to maximize employment and growth.

If fiscal and monetary policy are recommitted to full employment objectives, then other methods must be used to eliminate inflation. The plan to end inflation would specify a tolerable rate of disinflation, in the sense that it would not cause default rates on mortgages and other consumer debts to exceed historic norms; nor would it force contraction upon businesses anywhere within the wide range of normal wage contracts and debt financing. Aside from the detail underlying such a calculation, the plan would be simple, compared to the intricate plans prepared in France. Only a handful of variables would be specified for each year of the plan: the average rate of change of all prices and all wages; the growth of labor, capital per worker, output per worker, and thus total real output; and the growth of government spending and taxes, the levels of money, credit, and interest rates.

This might seem too simple to be called a plan. It will especially disappoint economists, civil servants, and others who are remunerated for compiling and then interpreting or mystifying complex plans. It is quite like the very general principles that were invoked to justify the Kennedy administration's guidelines. Indeed, so far the plan I have described is very similar to the economics of the early 1960s, including a first-priority commitment to high employment.

As with the Kennedy guidelines, the arithmetic relation between planned prices and wages depends on the growth of productivity. If wages grow as fast as prices plus output per worker, then the division between labor income and property income will be maintained in constant proportions. If the plan assumes excessively optimistic increases in labor productivity, businesses will correctly view this as justifying excessive growth of wages at the expense of profits. If no increases in productivity are assumed, this would amount to asking workers to accept a freeze on real wages for the duration of the plan, with all the benefits of any increased productivity going to employers.

Everything examined in this book suggests that weaker productivity performance since the mid-1960s was partly a result of inflation itself and of low levels of economic growth and utilization. The virtual disappearance of productivity growth from 1973 to 1982 was almost certainly a consequence of the OPEC price shocks. In that case, we can expect a resumption of near normal productivity growth in the 1980s once we re-establish healthy levels of employment and growth. A fair compromise might be to assume initial growth of output per hour worked at a rate of 2 percent a year, compared to 0.6 percent after 1973 and about 2.5 percent a year in the happy quarter-century preceding. After a few years under the plan, productivity assumptions would be periodically revised to reflect actual experience.

This productivity assumption, combined with a labor force growing a little over 1 percent a year, implies annual growth of real GNP just over 3 percent in the 1980s, after a reasonably high level of employment has been reached. Tax and spending policies in the plan should be consistent with this rate of real growth. Finally, tax policy and interest rates can be altered to adjust the incentives for investment so that the increase in capital per worker is at least equal to the apparent rate required to achieve the planned increase in output per worker. If labor productivity grows faster than the planned level because of higher-than-planned growth of capital per worker, the extra return to employers will compensate them for the extra investment. However, if labor productivity grows much faster or slower than planned for some other, unaccountable reasons, then it will be necessary to promptly revise the productivity assumptions to call for a faster deceleration of prices in the case of above-average productivity growth, or of wages in the case of productivity disappointment.

I have been describing only the "benign" aspects of an indicative plan. They are even more vague than the Kennedy guidelines. Accordingly, they would interfere even less with the efficient functions of prices in markets. And they would be even

less effective, especially as weapons to roll back a severe inflation rather than to merely contain a mild one. Everyone could
agree that this is a dandy plan for removing inflation with all of
its costs and burdens, while imposing practically no disadvantage on anyone. That is if everyone conformed to the plan. But
who would want to be first? If no one followed, such a leader
would suffer reduced wages or reduced profits and all for
naught. Everybody would be better off if everybody conformed; but those who take the lead might be punished, while
those who lag behind might be rewarded.

What could be more logical than for the government that has
taken the lead in preparing the plan to be the first to declare its
intention of acting as if it believed the plan? And what could be
more powerful? Governments are the dominant force in the
American economy. They account for 16 percent of all the jobs
in the United States. Government adherence to the plan would
mean that pay for these workers increased at the planned rate.
Governments purchase more than 10 percent of all the goods
sold in America. These purchases are concentrated in the federal government and concentrated again in the Department of
Defense. If a disinflation plan were seriously implemented, the
Department of Defense would stop the practice of paying its
contractors their costs plus a fixed profit margin. Instead it
would pay the planned rate of inflation in material inputs and
unit labor costs plus an appropriate profit.

Governments' roles as employers and purchasers do not exhaust their economic importance. Governments also transfer
directly to individuals an amount equal to 11 percent of GNP,
which has been taxed or borrowed from other individuals. This
is money well spent. There is evidence that the recipients spend
all of it promptly, which can be taken as evidence of need. In
any case, it means that these transfers are translated into effective demand that creates or sustains employment. Transfer payments are concentrated in the federal government, and concentrated again in Social Security. Since Social Security is already
indexed to inflation, there is an obvious possibility of gearing
payments to the contemporaneous rate of planned inflation
rather than to the observed rate of past inflation. In a similar

fashion, unemployment benefits could be geared to the planned level of wages, and many other categories of transfer payments could be similarly adjusted.

Government is also ubiquitously important as a regulator of market prices and practices. In many instances, such as telephone services and electric power, prices are regulated because monopoly conditions do not permit the market to set an efficient price. There is no compelling argument in such cases not to set the regulated rate on the basis of planned labor costs, thus imposing the planned level of wages on the regulated monopolies and their workers. In other regulated industries, like banking and insurance, there is no reason why the regulatory agencies could not use their discretion to encourage conformity with the plan's guidelines.

We have now entered an area of admittedly repugnant government interference. And while we are there, I might as well acknowledge that much of what has already been proposed depends on equally repugnant coercion. Two thirds of government employment and close to half of government purchases of goods and regulation of prices is accounted for by the fifty states and their tens of thousands of subdivisions. Yet only the federal government has the means and motive to develop a comprehensive anti-inflation program. But the federal government has ample means, repeatedly tested, to make local governments dance to its plan. In 1981, local governments received more than $90 billion, or more than one fifth of their total revenues, from the federal government. By threatening to withhold only small fractions of this flow, Washington has managed to impose its 55-mph preferred speed limit and its partiality for right turns at red lights on all of the fifty states. Washington also had little difficulty in obtaining local government cooperation with the "voluntary" Phase II of the Nixon controls or with the Carter guidelines. The federal government also has coercive powers, which it has employed previously, to obtain compliance from educational and other tax-exempt institutions that depend on government contracts, grants, or exemptions.

Ronald Reagan has repeatedly made clear that he is opposed to this kind of coercion. I wholeheartedly agree that it violates the spirit and intention of the Constitution. Still, I am a pragmatist. I think it would have been better to end inflation with some blood of ideological purity on the floor than with the corpse of the entire economy in the same place.

Moreover, none of these proposed acts of government can be effected by imperial edict. Public employees and their unions would have to be persuaded to accept the planned rate of wage increase at all levels of government. The large constituency that fiercely protects Social Security benefits would have to be persuaded that actual inflation was as likely to be below the planned rate as above it, before they would permit payments adjusted at a planned rather than the actual rate. An enormous array of federal and local legislators, executives, and regulatory agencies would have to be educated, wooed, cajoled, and persuaded that their constituencies were well-served by the plan. Once it is understood that nearly everyone gains from higher output and employment with the same division of benefits and no inflation, the basis exists for a cooperative, national effort to debate and formulate the planned reductions in speed limits for inflation. Thereafter, expecting those who exist on the public's favor and bounty to abide by its speed limits is no more autocratic than setting the traffic lights along a city street to synchronize with a legal and safe rate of progress.

17

Undoing Depression

As one studies the great depression that scourged the
Western world during the 1930s, the question inevitably arises: Could it happen again? Could the economies
of these nations slide into such a deep depression and
remain so depressed for a decade or more? The answer
must surely be, "No, not unless the governments of
those nations are plagued by some sort of political
deadlock that prevents them from taking the actions
that we know can shorten a depression and induce
recovery . . .

Of course, it is not inevitable that we shall in fact
achieve an almost continuous state of high employment
and output. New generations, ignorant of the tragedies
of a great depression, may fail to act in time.

LESTER V. CHANDLER
America's Greatest Depression (1970)

The dangers we face in the 1980s are, as always, more the effect
of ideas than adverse circumstances. As a welter of transcen-
dental economic doctrines first garner popular faith and then
flounder, it becomes more difficult to keep track of what is veri-
fied. As cures for inflation, we have seen that monetarism is a
dangerous snake medicine and supply side economics a mere
placebo. Controls, whether mandatory or voluntary, attack
only the symptoms of inflation. And precisely when the disease
advances to the stage where inflation is the cause of more inflation, controls even lose most of their symptomatic effectiveness.

Any attack on inflation through a Keynesian restriction of
demand, whether monetary or fiscal, has a small and delayed
effect on prices compared to its large and immediate negative
effect on real product and income. It is necessary, as I argued in

181

the last chapter, to attack inflation with some means other than those that merely remove the foundations of prosperity. The Reagan administration implied that the remedy for inflation involved eliminating only the surfeits of Keynesianism rather than its essentials. In chapter 3, we saw that the barest minimum of Keynesian success might already have inflationary consequences. However deep or shallow the surgery, it affects employment before it affects inflation. Even if the original causes of inflation could be clearly distinguished, eliminating them decades after the fact is no more an effective response to inflation than unplugging the offending appliance is an efficacious solution for a blown fuse.

A solution in the common interest requires common support over a number of years. A resurgence of the belief that the interplay of unregulated selfish interests yields an optimal array of social results has further weakened our willingness to enlist in a communal effort.

Meanwhile, we are lurching toward depression in an atmosphere where we might easily forget that we *do* know how to avert depressions or escape them. The ideology of individualism has been reinforced in the 1980s by experience that confounds the simplistic Keynesian model. In 1980 and 1981, we experienced another severe concurrence of high unemployment and high inflation. Then, in 1982, the federal deficit went to an all-time record while unemployment went to a forty-year high. Why didn't the large deliberate Reagan deficits produce growth in output and employment as was expected by many critics and supporters of the supply side tax cuts?

The rest of this chapter concerns answers to this question and their implications for policy. We began (chapters 1, 2, 3) with a review of the appropriate principles. The immediate determinant of the total value of GNP is the total value of demand. Excessive or inadequate demand is associated with similar deviations in the level of borrowing. A federal government deficit may counterbalance surpluses or subnormal deficits in other sectors. Alternatively, it may contribute all or part of an imbalance toward excessive borrowing and spending.

Once the change in the total value of GNP is determined, the division of that change between production and prices depends importantly on the composition of demand. If demand changes for goods whose supply can be readily expanded or contracted—like automobiles or running shoes—then the effect will be in the quantity produced and the quantity of workers and other resources employed in their production. In our economy, these goods tend to have fixed prices, which are changed infrequently. However, if demand changes for goods or services whose supply is inflexible for a period of time, then most of the change will be reflected in prices. These fixed-supply, flexible-price categories include agricultural products, industrial raw materials, labor in general, and especially, particular skill categories like schoolteachers or welders.

There is clearly no necessity for a large government deficit to coincide with high levels of employment. If the private economy sags, this will cause the deficit to grow, since federal revenues shrink in proportion to private incomes while unemployment compensation and other welfare categories of spending increase. However, since the spending increases and tax cuts are not as great as the decline in private incomes, the public deficit is only a partial offset to the drop in private deficits, and the economic contraction is not prevented. That is why peacetime federal deficits have invariably been largest at the troughs of recessions.

The only difference in 1982 was that a major portion of the jump in the deficit was attributed to tax cuts rather than to contraction of GNP. The supply siders had hoped and believed that these tax cuts, like the comparably timed Kennedy reductions of early 1964, would stimulate growth enough to forestall both recession and worsening deficits well beyond Reagan's first term. As the evidence of recession began to accumulate in the autumn of 1981, Ronald Reagan announced with apparent satisfaction that this was the first time a stimulative tax cut had been put in place before a recession began rather than after it was over. In truth, the huge 1981 tax cuts were more a cause of the ensuing recession than a successful prophylactic.

This surprising outcome was achieved by the circuitous route of the Federal Reserve. Some of those on the policy-making

Open Market Committee thought restrictive monetary policy was the divinely revealed path of righteousness. Others thought it was the logical and requested complement to the tax cuts. And perhaps a plurality believed it was a necessary if painful antidote to the inflationary dangers of "voodoo economics." For most of the latter group, the difficulties caused by high interest rates created the additional prospect of having something to trade with the Congress and White House in return for more appropriate policies; or, in the extreme, something with which to punish the irresponsible Republicans in the midterm elections.

Therefore, the tax cuts were followed by a declining economy, in part because they led to still higher interest rates. Interest rates discouraged more private borrowing and spending than the federal budget and deficit created. As we have seen, the buoyancy of borrowing and investment are functions of both interest rates and confidence that the federal government will maintain GNP at high levels so that investments will be profitable and debts repayable. A decade of disappointment had weakened this confidence. By its words and deeds, the Reagan administration damaged it further. A government that courts and tolerates severe unemployment as a cure for inflation is not likely to encourage high investment and rapid growth even with very large tax cuts.

Finally, we must look at the composition of changes in federal spending and taxes. The tax side is straightforward. The "Economic Recovery Tax Act of 1981"—never was legislation so inauspiciously named—provided nearly $60 billion in reduced taxes for calendar 1982. Of this amount, an estimated $45 billion was from the first two installments of the reductions in personal income tax rates. With its usual solicitude for the burdens of affluence, Congress took care to give taxpayers in the highest bracket their entire reduction at the beginning of 1982 (even more immediately for capital gains income) rather than making them wait with the lowly until the middle of 1984. While the maximum tax rate was cut from 70 percent to 50 percent, nothing was done to alter the increases in the Social Security tax rate and tax base that had already been legislated through the middle of this decade; nor was anything done to adjust the minimum exemptions from taxable income, at least not until a token adjustment becomes effective in 1985. As a result, the wealthiest 4 percent of the population received over 40 percent of the tax cuts for 1982, even though these families and individuals had been paying only about 23 percent of total income taxes and Social Security taxes.

One of the obvious truths of life, which is often doubted and debated by economists, is that those with relatively low incomes are inclined or required to spend all of them on current purchases, while those with relatively high incomes are inclined or required to devote substantial portions to various forms of saving and investment. A tax cut for the highest-income 4 percent will certainly have less impact on demand, production, and employment than the same cuts made available to the bottom 40 percent of the income scale. In effect, instead of taxing high-income households, the federal government agreed to borrow some of the money from the same sources. To that extent the tax cuts did nothing to increase employment.

The balance of the Reagan tax cuts were mostly in the liabilities of corporations and to a lesser extent in estate taxes. Since the estate tax reductions applied to portfolios of assets rather than to streams of income, their primary effect was also to have the government borrow from estates and heirs what it previously would have taken in taxes. The estimated reductions in corporate tax liabilities resulted from more generous allowances for depreciation of plant and equipment purchased in 1981 or later. However, reducing the tax on income earned from investment will not stimulate capital spending unless businesses believe that the new capital will generate an income to be taxed. Weak aggregate demand and high interest rates overwhelmed any possible investment stimulus from the revisions of depreciation.

To the considerable extent that these tax reductions did not contribute to demand, they did nothing to raise employment and incomes. The deficit ballooned in 1982, just as it had in previous recessions, not so much because the rate of taxation on incomes was lowered, but because the level of taxable income was lowered, while falling employment added to expenditures.

The composition of spending changes in the federal budget was also inappropriate for combating unemployment. In the budget, both as planned and as realized, the entire increase in the deficit was accounted for by increases in two categories of expenditures: net interest payments and defense spending. These increased about 10 percent faster than inflation, while all other budget categories fell by 2 percent after inflation.

If interest rates are elevated because of inflation, then the government's creditors must reinvest the "inflation premium" part of their interest receipts in the purchase of more government obligations just to preserve the purchasing power of their bond portfolios and their future stream of spendable interest. The inflation premium is really a return of the investors' principal. Only an accounting convention distinguishes between selling new debt to pay the inflation premium and selling new debt to retire the principal of old debt. The latter transaction does not add to the deficit. Clearly, neither event increases spending for goods and labor.

In actuality, interest rates were high in 1982 more because the Federal Reserve *made* them high than as a reflection of inflation. But it is the actuality as well, that most government debt is held by banks, insurance companies, pension funds, and wealthy individuals. These holders tend to reinvest all of their interest in new debt, whatever the rate of inflation. Borrowing money to pay interest on the debt is essentially the same thing as issuing new debt to the same institutions and individuals who already hold the existing debt. Clearly, this will not enlarge demand in the same way as borrowing a similar amount of money to buy locomotives or to subsidize health care.

In its obsessive equation of national security with the dollars spent for that purpose, the Reagan administration has substituted the implicit standard of more bucks for the bang in place of the slogan offered by Eisenhower's Secretary of Defense, Charles Wilson, "more bang for the buck." As a matter of policy, the increased allocations for personnel have been used to raise incomes, not employment. To the extent that military hardware requires specialized skills, facilities, and components that are already strained close to capacity, the remainder of the defense increases also adds to the price of production rather than the volume.

Therefore, the categories of spending that have been enlarged do little or nothing for production and employment, especially in contrast to the categories that have been contracted. These spending and taxing decisions, coupled with extraordinary interest rates and declarations that the federal government no longer was committed to using monetary or fiscal policy to sustain a high level of demand, have had the effect of depressing private incomes, borrowing, and spending. A depressed GNP has been the primary reason for successive, record deficits.

The Keynesian prescriptions for depression were first oversimplified, then somewhat misapplied, then confronted with circumstances that Keynes had not anticipated or understood, and finally rejected out of ignorance. It is worthwhile to restate the basic principles that can be successfully applied to preventing or reversing a depression. Used with care and skill, they can minimize the possibilities of creating or increasing inflation. For now, I assume that their reapplication occurs simultaneously with effective anti-inflation measures of the sort described in the last chapter, or in the midst of a depression so severe that inflation has already been killed in the pandemic disaster.

The first principle is to create total demand sufficiently large to employ a high percentage of the nation's labor and capital resources. As we have seen, the size of the federal government's deficit has little to do with whether or not this objective has been achieved. Lower interest rates help by encouraging more private spending, financed with more private borrowing. However, depressed conditions may make business investment unattractive at even a zero rate of interest; unemployed workers will not borrow money to buy new cars and houses whatever the charge. Even those who enjoy present prosperity may be deterred from borrowing to buy additional assets if they lack confidence in the maintenance of future demand and employment. Finally, there are objective limits to the practical demand for many investments financed with borrowed money. The auto industry is not going to borrow to expand capacity to fifteen million cars a year, no matter how full the level of employment or low the rate of interest might be. Similarly, for purely demographic reasons, there is probably no monetary policy stimulative enough to push residential and commercial construction as high in the 1980s as it was in the 1970s.

Economists have an aphorism for these problems, as they do for so much else. Easing monetary policy when nobody wants to increase borrowing is like "pushing on a string." The alternative is for fiscal policy to get on the other side of things and "pull." Pulling with tax cuts will succeed if the money that is not taken in taxes ends up being spent by the taxpayer. However, it is obviously futile to cut the taxes of unemployed workers and struggling businesses who already have no income to be taxed.

If money and taxes are not sufficient, the infallible solution is for the government to spend whatever is necessary to employ idle workers and resources. It is not necessary for the government to hire all of the unemployed directly. For every dollar that the government adds to GNP or person it adds to employment, total GNP and total employment will go up by about two dollars or workers. This is because most of the initial dollar of new income is spent to become additional income, most of which is again spent, and so on. As a result, the government will gain about 40¢ in taxes out of the new $2.00 of GNP, and it will save about 30¢ in unemployment and welfare costs. Thus, about 70¢ out of the dollar originally spent will come back in revenues or savings.

Government demand must be focused on output that can be expanded by using unemployed workers and capacity, not on goods and skills that are already fully used. In the latter case, inflation will be added to our burdens, when the object was to remove unemployment. It is best to have the government buy goods and services that will expand the quality of our lives and be of lasting economic value. An economist may shed some light on the second criterion. The first can be satisfactorily achieved only through a process that is open, informed, and truly democratic. In what follows, I mix my professional advice as an economist with my personal contribution as a human being to the debate over proper public purposes.

In the first place, we need not feel compelled to spend money solely because we know the expenditure will be effective against unemployment. As I shall demonstrate in a moment, there are ample methods to eradicate serious unemployment and achieve worthwhile goals at the same time. Even though we know that Social Security recipients will spend all of any additional benefits, thus maximizing the employment effects, there is no reason not to set benefit levels to balance what is fair or generous against the burden on present taxpayers, without regard for the impact on total demand.

Throughout the United States, public transportation systems are in need of repair and expansion. In the East, intraurban systems are badly decayed, while in the West, they were often not taken very far to begin with. Interurban rail transportation is being liquidated now that it has become a public function. Expenditure in these areas would clearly direct demand into precisely those segments of the economy that have the most unused labor and capital capacity: steel, machinery, cement, transportation equipment, and construction.

Improved public transportation systems have direct economic benefits. The provision of a transportation system is one of the supply functions that belongs to government in classical theory. Otherwise young adults may find themselves in the position of needing to own automobiles *before* they can take jobs. Alternatively, employers might have to provide private buses to transport employees from their homes to work and back, as already happens in places like Boston, or stores might create systems to gather and return customers. Mass transit systems, on the other hand, enjoy economies of scale that lower costs.

Other benefits are more difficult to measure and to locate precisely. Public transportation systems are usually more energy efficient than their private alternatives and are often less polluting. Most of the pedestrians and irritated drivers on clogged urban streets and expressways would be very happy if everyone else decided to take the bus or subway. Merchants have discovered that carless streets are good for business. But these are not easy combinations of considerations to add up and compare. There is probably no technocratically decisive way of determining how much to spend on subways or buses and how much to support the development of private automobiles.

If all the costs that can be measured (building, maintaining, policing, and lighting highways; buying, repairing, replacing, garaging, insuring, gasing, and oiling autos; plus many more costs and a comparable list for the public system alternative) are added up and divided by appropriate figures for passenger miles, the resulting cost estimates are still not reliable. As we saw in the case of oil, a price does not always convey much useful information about costs or benefits. These calculations have no room for the costs of noise and exhaust, for the benefits to merchants, the value of reduced fatalities, the wages of less time wasted, the worth of energy resources saved to the world economy and future generations. Nor, on the other side, do they price the inconvenience of waiting for the bus, walking home in the rain, kids who smoke on the subway and blast passengers with their radios.

In principle, all of this can be measured or priced. In practice we are left with a matter of judgment. Mine is that everyone's life would be better if our public system of transportation were better. The quality of such a system is more a function of our determination and culture than it is of some immutable laws of economics.

A serious reconstruction and extension of our public transportation might involve spending about $500 billion for the 20 largest cities and another $500 billion for the revival of Amtrak and provision for smaller towns and cities. Spread over ten years, this would imply an average annual increment to demand of $100 billion (1982 dollars). This, in turn, is close to what is needed to restore full employment. In any case, the considerations that support an investment in public transportation apply equally to a number of other areas: waste disposal, water supply, parks, recreation, public health and medicine, plus much more.

Education is not on the preceding list because of two complications that warrant some discussion. First, for the same demographic reasons that have depressed housing, the education "industry" is depressed. There are underutilized and unemployed grade schools and college dormitories, teachers, professors, and textbook editors. Second, experience in recent decades has decisively proved that more money does not buy better education, in the same way that it does not buy more national security. Both have more to do with a state of mind and sense of purpose than with the money to provide teachers and textbooks or troops and ammunition.

Our problem well into the 1990s is to use our existing educational resources to make investments for the future, rather than to invest in more school buildings. One obvious possibility springs from these facts. Unemployment has been greatest among teen-agers, blue-collar workers, and those, including the foregoing, with limited educations in math, science, and other disciplines that are particularly relevant to the new technologies. Why not use unemployed educators and school buildings to impart these critical skills to unemployed construction and auto workers? Such a renewal of the dying federal support for job-skill training and retraining would provide an optimal impact on current employment and on future economic well-being also.

Surely we are better off as taxpayers if we pay teachers to teach and workers to study new skills, rather than give both a meager dole for being unemployed. The present atmosphere would be more tolerable in every aspect if such a policy were vigorously pursued. As already noted, every dollar spent for these happy results would end up costing taxpayers only about 30¢.

18

The Economy
of Intelligence

> One can easily envisage a situation in which technolog-
> ical progress permits output to increase at a high rate
> without *any* additions to the stock of capital goods . . .
>   It may be that the essential investments are largely in
> human beings, the active agents in society, not in sticks,
> stones, and metal.
>
> SIMON KUZNETS
> *Toward a Theory of Economic Growth* (1953)

If this book has had central themes, they are that the economy
is a supremely social concept, subject to social control and decision; and that ideas have always been the critical determinant
of economic affairs. We have the ability, and ample motive, to
ensure the productive employment of existing labor and capital. Since money itself is also a creation of the social imagination, it can and should be subjected to social control. Money is
created when loans are made to finance the accumulation of
new assets that will produce a flow of future benefits. The paper
money thus created is exchanged and re-exchanged for present
goods and services. There is therefore an inevitable social interest in the validity of these future prospects. When that interest
is most successfully expressed, the money created by private
lending is socialized. Privately created money is wrapped in the
government's flag and guarantees. In return, the private creation of money is subjected to rules and regulations that protect
the social interest against greed and fraud.

  The notion that everything has its price is not a scientific discovery about the nature of the world, but rather, an idea about
how to organize the world. In our society that idea has been

192

pushed to and beyond its limits. It has much to do with the triumphs of modern economic development. But it also yields that grim calculus which optimizes the ratio between the costs of various nuclear war capacities and strategies and the "price" of the probable lives lost times their quantity.

It is intrinsic to economies that are competitive or growing or changing that supply and demand will almost always be out of balance, both in particular markets and in the entire economy. The idea that we are honor-bound to endure the correction of these imbalances, without any application of collective intelligence and regardless of the extent or duration of disequilibrium, is not based on a revelation of eternal truth. It is an idea that long ago was proven false by experience. Its reappearance is due to a combination of our social atomization and a general decline in our ability to reason from evidence.

At the time that powerful ideas have transformed our society and brought new techniques of production to different industries, the increasing breadth and depth of knowledge has made continuous contributions to our economic advance. If there is a universal prerequisite for modern economic development it is education, with its attendant skills and attitudes. Edward F. Denison, an economist skilled at such measurements, has calculated that advances in knowledge plus increased education of workers contributed three to six times more to twentieth-century economic growth than the growth of all tangible capital goods owned by households, businesses, and governments. John W. Kendrick, another accomplished measurer of economic inputs and outputs, has calculated our "inventory" of knowledge and learned abilities from the costs of "producing" it. He finds, as have many others, that these assets earn a yield that is more than competitive with the yields from factories or power plants. Net additions to this "inventory" have been twice as large as our additions to the stock of buildings, machines, houses, automobiles, and other tangible goods. By the early 1980s, our stock of knowledge and ideas was more valuable, in Kendrick's sense, than all of the capital goods we had produced and accumulated.

What truly distinguishes the United States and other developed countries from our less-developed counterparts is what is in our minds rather than some accumulation of brick and steel. Schooling has been an essential and growing component of economic activity and contributor to economic progress, one of the great luxuries that affluence affords. Knowledge and education are far more widely dispersed than household financial assets or corporate buildings and machinery. The growth in the relative importance of knowledge has been the decisive factor in the democratization of wealth and income. And we are not through yet. The importance of microcomputers, telecommunications, and scientific knowledge in the major techniques of the next century suggests that advanced economies will become increasingly producers and consumers of ideas instead of material objects.

This Economy of Intelligence is a future that should be a cause only for rejoicing and renewed aspiration. We have ample ability to understand and guide it with an intelligent economics.

Appendix
Notes and Sources
Index

Appendix

The Past Relationships Between
Inflation, Money, and Borrowing

This appendix is only for those readers who have been properly trained not to believe what they read, and who therefore desire some proof of the assertion made in chapter 1 that debt and changes in debt bear a more reliable and consistent relationship to GNP and price changes than do any of the various definitions of money. I will attempt to demonstrate this fact as simply as possible. However, I do assume that the reader of this appendix has some familiarity with economics and statistics. We shall see that while money sometimes exhibits an independently significant relationship to incomes and inflation, the magnitude of borrowing relative to GNP is a far more reliable and consistent explanation of the growth in GNP and prices, as well as a more plausible one.

Table 1 presents some basic information about the value of GNP (in current dollars) relative to the year-end quantities of money and debt. The measures of money are M1, which consists of currency in circulation, demand deposits, and other deposits that are readily available for payments by check; and M2, which consists of M1 plus savings accounts, money market funds, and other forms of money that are slightly less convenient as means of payment and that typically provide better interest returns than the components of M1.

The measure of debt is the total, net, public, and private, debt issued by U.S. households, businesses, and governments. It is "net" in the sense that it excludes loans between households or related businesses and some government debt owned by governments. The years 1916 through 1976 have been selected for analysis, because this debt series is published on a consistent basis for these sixty-one years. The analysis offered in chapter 2 suggests that a more appropriate measure of debt would include borrowing within sectors, since this leads directly to more spending; while it should exclude borrowing by financial insti-

Table 1   The Ratio of GNP to Money and Debt: 1916–1976

Year	$\dfrac{GNP^1}{M1^2}$	$\dfrac{GNP^1}{M2^2}$	$\dfrac{GNP^1}{Debt^3}$
1916	3.05	2.12	.588
1926	3.78	2.24	.573
1936	2.63	1.81	.457
1946	1.92	1.47	.526
1956	3.06	2.22	.600
1966	4.35	1.58	.560
1976	5.52	1.47	.512
61-year sample: s.d. ÷ mean[4]	.261	.165	.130

1. GNP: 1916–1938, U.S. Bureau of the Census, *Historical Statistics of the United States* (Washington, D.C.: U.S. Government Printing Office, 1975), Part 1, p. 224, Series F-1; 1939–1976, *Economic Report of the President* (Washington, D.C.: U.S. Government Printing Office, 1982), p. 233.

2. M1, M2: Figures are end of December before 1946 and the average for December for 1946 and subsequent years. 1916–1958: Milton Friedman and Anna J. Schwartz, *Monetary Statistics of the United States* (New York: National Bureau of Economic Research, 1970), pp. 17–47. 1959–1976: *Economic Report of the President*, 1982, p. 303.

3. Debt: 1916–1954: *Historical Statistics*, Part 2, p. 989, Series X-393. 1955–1964: *Survey of Current Business*, May 1970, p. 14. 1965–1976: *Survey of Current Business*, July 1977, p. 15.

4. This row presents the standard deviation of all 61 observations divided by their arithmetic average.

tutions, since this is only indirectly related to more demand for goods and services.

The numbers, shown at ten-year intervals, are representative of each of the entire series. The first entry in the table (1916: GNP/M1) indicates that for every dollar of M1 in existence at the end of 1916, GNP in that year amounted to $3.05. A similar interpretation applies to every other entry in the table until the last row. It is apparent that the relationship of GNP to M1 has been most unstable; to M2 reasonably stable; and to debt, most nearly constant. The first two columns are measures of what are normally called the "velocities" of M1 and M2.

The drop of nearly 50 percent in the velocity of M1 from 1926 through 1946 implies that GNP would have fallen a similar amount if the money supply had been maintained at a constant level over these two decades. Conversely, a growth of M1 equal to 3.5 percent a year was consistent with virtually no change in GNP from 1926 to 1946. The near tripling of M1 velocity in the first three decades after World War II suggests that GNP would have grown more than 3.5 percent a year even if there had been a constant level of M1.

The range of these seven numbers (the largest minus the smallest) divided by their arithmetic averages is 1.04, .42, and .26, for M1, M2, and debt, respectively. The final row confirms this ranking of the relative stability of the ratios with a presentation of the standard deviation divided by the mean over the entire sixty-one-year sample. Again, the smaller the entry, the more constant the respective ratio. Benjamin Friedman ("The Relative Stability of Money and Credit 'Velocities' in the United States," in *The Changing Roles of Debt and Equity in Financing U.S. Capital Formation,* Benjamin Friedman, ed. [New York: National Bureau of Economic Research, 1983]) has confirmed these relative degrees of stability for the years 1953–1978, using the preferable measure of all debt issued (including intrasectoral loans) minus the debt of financial institutions. Friedman's analysis also considers M3 and the Monetary Base, each of which also exhibits less stable relationships to GNP than does the debt total.

Monetarists have dealt with the instability of the M1:GNP relationship by trying to account for the changes over time in the institutional arrangements (pay periods, credit cards, etc.) that affect the amount of economic activity that can be supported by a given amount of cash and demand deposits. Alternatively, they have sought to use M2 as the appropriate definition of money, since the relationship to GNP is less variable. For examples of these approaches see the footnotes for pages 5 and 6 in this volume.

However, the real question is not whether money or debt has grown at roughly the same rate as GNP over the decades, thus preserving a constant ratio; but whether the growth of these financial aggregates is in some way a cause, or the measure of a cause, of a component of the growth of GNP. One way to assess these possibilities is to examine the degree of statistical correlation between changes in GNP and the contemporaneous or prior growth of the different money and debt totals.

Table 2 summarizes just such a regression analysis for each of the three financial variables compared with the growth of GNP. The significance of each variable is estimated in equations of identical structure

Table 2 Alternative Regressions to Account for the Growth of Nominal GNP

Sample Observations: 1922–1976

Basic Regression Equation:

$$\ln(GNP/GNP_{-1}) = C + a(X) + a1(X_{-1}) + a2(X_{-2}) + a3(X_{-3})$$
$$+ a4(X_{-4}) + a5(X_{-5}) + t(Time)$$

Equation	X is:	C	a	a1	a2	t	Adjusted R^2	Standard Error
1.	$\ln(M1/M_{-1})$	−.013 (1.04)	.541 (3.97)**	.610 (4.06)**	−.284 (1.89)*	.001 (2.39)*	.57	.056
2.	$\ln(M2/M2_{-1})$	.003 (.14)	.523 (3.93)**	.342 (2.47)**	−.116 (.83)	.0003 (.50)	.37	.067
3.	$\ln\left(1 + \dfrac{Debt - Debt_{-1}}{GNP}\right)$	.015 (.98)	1.05 (7.64)**	−.029 (.17)	−.459 (2.78)**	.0002 (.42)	.67	.049

Columns C through t headed by "Estimated Coefficients".

Notes and Sources:

ln signifies the natural logarithm of whatever follows in parentheses. Subscripts, $_{-1}$, $_{-2}$, etc., after a variable indicate the value of that number one year earlier, two years earlier, etc.

The numbers in parentheses under the estimated coefficients are the absolute values of the t-statistics.

** indicates statistical significance at the 1 percent level; * at the 5 percent level.

Time is the number of the year, with 1922 = 0.

For the data sources, see the notes to Table 1.

from observations over the fifty-five-year period 1922–1976. The effects of money and debt changes are considered for the year of measured GNP growth and each of the five preceding years. The monetarist literature, mentioned above, has suggested that lags as long as five years are necessary to fully account for the influences of money on GNP. Variables lagged more than two years were not individually significant in any of the three regressions; and therefore they are not shown in the table. The addition of changes from three, four, and five years earlier did eliminate a statistically significant tendency of all three regression equations to oscillate systematically between overestimating and underestimating the growth of GNP without substantially changing the adjusted estimates of variance accounted for.

A constant term and time as an independent variable are both included because they are needed to account for the changing ratio of GNP to M1 discussed above and shown in Table 1. The estimated coefficients for time and the constant term in the first equation suggest that GNP was increasing about 1.3 percent a year less than the movement of M1 alone would warrant in 1922, and about 5.1 percent a year more than the same calculation would indicate for 1976. (This calculation is based on the unrounded coefficients, while those in the table have been shown to the third decimal place only.)

In the first two equations, the rate of change of GNP is related to the rate of change of M1 and M2, respectively. This is in accord with the theory of monetarism as explained in chapter 1. In the third equation, the growth of GNP is related to the change in outstanding debt relative to the value of GNP. This is a rough measure of the proportion of GNP that was accounted for by deficit spending—the relevant indicator suggested by the view I have presented in chapter 2.

The estimated proportion of the variance in the growth of nominal GNP that can be accounted for by synchronous movements in each of the financial aggregates, its lagged values, and time trends is about 57 percent in the case of M1, 37 percent in the case of M2, and 67 percent for debt. The performances of M1 and M2 in Table 1 are reversed. While the ratio of GNP to M1 is extremely variable over time, there is a fairly precise correspondence between the change in M1 and the change in GNP. The story is reversed for M2. A steady average ratio turns out to be an entirely unsteady correspondence between changes in M2 and GNP. The weakness of this correspondence is not fully clear from Table 2, since M1 (which is significantly related to changes in GNP) is also a component of M2. In any case, Table 1 indicates that the relationship between debt and GNP is more reliable than the relationship between M1 or M2 and GNP, while Table 2 indicates that the relationship between the change in debt and the change in GNP is also more reliable than the analogous relationships involving the changes in M1 or M2.

The poor performance of M2 in Table 2 is not surprising. The savings accounts, money market funds, and other liquid assets that make up the bulk of M2 are precisely the places where wealth is invested instead of or until the purchase of stocks and bonds or houses and autos. They are safe havens in times of uncertainty and logical parking places for funds diverted from the purchase of durable goods. Therefore, although the long-run relationship between M2 and GNP may be stable, in the short run money tends to flow into M2 just as GNP is turning down and to come out of M2 to purchase houses, cars, and other borrowers' debt (see chapter 2) just as GNP is turning up. For example, from 1965 through 1981, the growth rates of GNP and M2 changed in opposite directions in eleven out of sixteen years. Even a five-year moving-average growth rate of M2 changed in the opposite direction from GNP growth in half of these sixteen years.

The significant correlation between changes in M1 and changes in nominal GNP survives statistical scrutiny. If the current and the first two lagged values of the M1 and debt variables used in Table 2 are employed simultaneously to estimate the growth of nominal GNP, both the current value of debt increase relative to GNP and the previous year's growth rate of M1 remain significant at the 1 percent level. Other debt and money observations are of more marginal significance. The three debt variables, with t-ratios ranging from 1.24 to 6.02, are substantially more significant than the three money variables, with t-ratios between .85 and 3.2. Still, to give the monetarists their due, there is some fluctuation in either the demand for or the supply of currency and checking accounts, which occurs independently of the debt creation process and which bears a strong connection to changes in nominal GNP about one year later.

One more point is worth mentioning. In the equation just described, the three equations in Table 2, and many more regressions which I have not described, the coefficients of all money and debt variables lagged two years and are consistently negative and usually significant. It is unlikely that there is something about the movements of M1, M2, or debt that causes GNP to move in the opposite direction two years later. On the other hand, since all the data have been measured in a crude and arbitrary fashion (year-over-year changes in GNP and end-of-year to end-of-year changes in money and debt) it is very likely that more finely calibrated inflections and effects have been lost. Since the average half-life of a business cycle is about two years (see chapter 11), there is an occasional chance for the lagged variable to pick up some explanatory power when the arbitrary annual periods obscure the more contemporaneous relation.

I turn now to the relation between the rate of inflation (or deflation) and changes in the same three financial variables. Monetarism asserts that the growth rate of potential, real GNP is relatively constant—say somewhere between 2.5 percent and 4 percent a year since 1916. Therefore, the price level will be stable, rising, or falling as the growth of the money supply is appropriate, too high, or too low for this amount of real growth. My argument in chapter 2 suggests that inflation is a function of the ratio of spending (effective demand) to incomes. The ratio of net debt creation to GNP is, in turn, a good index of the relative strength of demand. Thus, inflation would be a direct function of the proportion of GNP financed by new debt creation. In addition, the analysis in chapter 6 suggests that previous inflation is itself an important, independent cause of further inflation.

A simple regression of price change against the previous year's price change for the sixty years, 1917–1976, accounts for an estimated 17 percent of inflation variability. Over the same sample, the growth of M2 accounts for 19 percent of price variance. A regression of price change against the rate of change in M1, the previous year's growth in M1, and a variable representing time, accounts for 28 percent of price variance. Finally, a simple regression of price change against the new debt portion of GNP accounts for 27 percent.

Table 3 reports two regressions in which these independent variables are allowed to complement one another and to compete in accounting for variations in price changes. In both regressions, borrowing relative to GNP, the previous year's inflation, and the growth rates of M1 and M2 are related to the change in the price level. In the first regression, data are considered for all sixty years from 1917 through 1976. The result is not much better than using only borrowing or only M1 to account for price variance. Only about one third of total variance is accounted for. Just the terms representing the momentum of inflation and the growth of M1 are statistically significant; and then only at the 5 percent level.

The second regression in Table 3 repeats the same analysis, excluding the twelve years in the sample during which World Wars I and II, or their aftermaths, caused maximum disturbances. The result is a substantial improvement and a tolerably good accounting for the fluctuations in the rate of change of prices. Price change momentum and the growth in debt relative to GNP are now both highly significant. The constant term is nearly significant at the 5 percent level. However, both money effects are statistically indistinguishable from *zero* effect. The coefficient of M2 even appears with a negative sign.

Table 4 presents average rates of change for prices, M1, and M2 and average rates of the change in debt relative to GNP, over seven subperiods of the interval from 1916 through 1976. Readers with no knowledge of regression equations may nonetheless be able to see from this table that different rates of inflation from one subperiod to another are more closely related to different proportions of GNP financed with debt than they are to the growth rates of M1 or M2. In the

**Table 3   Regressions of the Rate of Price Change Against
the Growth Rates of Money and the Change in Debt
Relative to GNP**

The dependent variable is $\dot{P}$ = ln(GNP Deflator/GNP Deflator$_{-1}$)

Sample Period	Constant	$\dfrac{\text{Debt}}{\text{GNP}}$	$\dot{P}_{-1}$	$\dot{M}1$	$\dot{M}2$	Adjusted R^2	Standard Error
		Estimated Coefficients Against					
1917–1976	−.007	.13	.29	.24	.05	.34	.050
	(.67)	(1.05)	(2.38)*	(1.74)*	(.33)		
1922–1939	−.010	.26	.38	.07	−.03	.61	.027
&	(1.65)	(3.39)**	(4.62)**	(.77)	(.44)		
1947–1976							

Notes and Sources:
Debt/GNP, $\dot{M}1$, and $\dot{M}2$ are the variables defined as X in Table 2, for equations 3, 1, and 2 respectively. For the meaning of all other symbols see the notes to Table 2. The GNP Deflator for 1916–1938 is from *Historical Statistics*, Part 1, p. 224, Series F-5, spliced to data for the period 1939–1981 from the *Economic Report of the President*, 1982, p. 237. For the sources of all other data, see the notes to Table 1.

1930s, M1 *increased* by 38 percent, while the price level *fell* by 15 percent. During World War II, M1 and M2 grew about twice as fast as they had during similar periods of inflation before and after, while the ratio of borrowing to GNP was similar. M2 moves quite contrary to inflation since the end of World War II. None of the variables offers much explanation for the relatively low inflation experienced from the mid-1950s through the mid-1960s.

Regression analysis confirms these observations. The growth of M1 accounts for an estimated 31 percent of the variance of price behavior among these seven intervals, while the debt variable accounts for a substantially stronger 78 percent. Growth of M2 has a negative relation to inflation.

Table 4 suggests that M1 might provide a better explanation of inflation if attention is confined to the years after 1946. This is indeed the

**Table 4   Average Rates of Change of Prices and Money,
and Average Levels of Debt Financing Over Multi-Year Intervals**

Interval	Average Annual Change in:			Average Annual Increase in Debt
	Prices	M1	M2	GNP
1916–1922	5.7%	6.5%	7.9%	12.5%
1922–1929	.1	2.1	3.7	7.9
1929–1939	−1.6	3.3	1.2	−2.1
1939–1946	6.3	16.7	15.4	16.8
1946–1956	3.6	2.4	2.9	9.1
1956–1966	2.0	2.4	9.8	11.2
1966–1976	5.6	6.0	9.3	16.6

Notes and Sources:
For the data sources see the notes to Tables 3 and 1. The first three columns are compound rates of change. The final column is the geometric average of the annual figures.

case. For the years 1947–1976, regressing the change in the price level against the same year's change in M1 produces an adjusted R^2 of .53; the same year's debt ratio produces an improved .55; and the use of only the previous year's growth of M1 yields the highest ratio of all at .59. Each of these regressions also includes the previous year's rate of price change, and this is the variable that accounts for the bulk of inflation variance. When lagged money growth and the current debt ratio both appear in a regression with lagged inflation, neither of them accounts for much; but, M1 is clearly the superior variable of the two in the post–World War II period.

A statistical analysis cannot ever prove anything. Rather, it is merely an efficient way of describing a set of facts. Sometimes the facts can disprove a theory by contradicting its expectations. The facts described in this appendix do not flatly contradict the monetarist position. They do suggest that purely monetary theory is a very incomplete and imperfect explanation of the forces that drive price changes. In addition they are more strongly consistent with the theories of aggregate deficit financing and the inertia of inflation, as presented in chapters 2 and 6.

Changes in M1 do bear a positive relationship to changes in prices, independent of changes in outstanding debt. The evidence presented here does not enable us to determine whether the fluctuations in M1 are themselves caused by changes in the "supply" of money, the demand for money, or some other factor of which M1 is only a symptom. The growth of M2 does seem most plausibly related to private decisions on the demand side. M2 increases the most when the demand to spend and invest is decreasing the most. The proportion of GNP financed with new debt relates to inflation quite plausibly if it is interpreted as an index of the aggregate excess demand expressed by all public and private sectors of the economy.

Notes and Sources

PART I

CHAPTER 1

5   Dallas S. Batten, "Inflation: The Cost-Push Myth," *Review,* Vol. 63, No. 6 (June/July 1981), Federal Reserve Bank of St. Louis, p. 22.

6   For evidence on the changing (and sometimes disappearing) lead time of money fluctuations over GNP fluctuations, see Keith M. Carlson, "Money, Inflation, and Economic Growth: Some Updated Reduced Form Results and Their Implications," *Review,* Vol. 62, No. 4 (April 1980), Federal Reserve Bank of St. Louis, pp. 13–19; Keith M. Carlson, "The Lag from Money to Prices," *Review,* Vol. 62, No. 8 (October 1980), Federal Reserve Bank of St. Louis, pp. 3–10; and Robert J. Gordon and James A. Wilcox, "Monetarist Interpretations of the Great Depression: An Evaluation and Critique" in *The Great Depression Revisited,* Karl Brunner, ed. (Boston/The Hague/London: Martinus Nijhoff, 1981), pp. 59–62.

CHAPTER 2

12   For median prices in the new and secondary single-family housing market, see Goldman Sachs, *The Pocket Chartroom,* pp. 15–16 of any recent monthly issue. For median family income, see *The Economic Report of the President* (Washington, D.C.: U.S. Government Printing Office, 1982), p. 264.

CHAPTER 3

17   John Maynard Keynes, *The Means to Prosperity* (London: Macmillan and Co., 1933).

18– The share of after-tax corporate profits in the GNP can be calculated
19   from *The Economic Report of the President* (Washington, D.C.: U.S. Government Printing Office, 1982), pp. 254 and 257. All of the other figures given are from Arthur M. Okun, "Measuring the Impact of the 1964 Tax Reduction," in *Perspectives on Economic Growth,* Walter W. Heller, ed. (New York: Random House, 1968), p. 36.

21   For an excellent discussion of the divergent paths pursued by the New Deal and suggested by Keynesian theory and Keynes himself, see Robert Lekachman, *The Age of Keynes* (New York: Random House, 1966), pp. 112–26.

24   John Maynard Keynes, *The General Theory of Employment, Interest, and Money* (New York: Harcourt, Brace, 1936), p. 296.

25   For data on the stability of corporate concentration, see Bureau of the Census, *Historical Statistics of the United States* (Washington, D.C.: U.S. Government Printing Office, 1975), Part 2, pp. 687, 914, 915; and the sources cited for those tables. More recent data appear in Lawrence J. White, "The Merger Wave: Is It a Problem?" *The Wall Street Journal,* December 11, 1981, p. 26.

26   John Kenneth Galbraith, *The Affluent Society* (Boston: Houghton Mifflin Co., 1958).

CHAPTER 4

29–
30   Most of the statistics on debt are compiled in Benjamin M. Friedman, "Postwar Changes in the American Financial Markets," in *The American Economy in Transition,* Martin Feldstein, ed. (Chicago: The University of Chicago Press, 1980), p. 18. More recent data are available in Henry Kaufman et al., *1982 Prospects for Financial Markets* (New York: Salomon Brothers Inc., 1982), p. 20.

32

Interval	Average Annual Growth of U.S. Consumption	
	Oil Products	Electricity
1945–1955	5.9%	8.7%
1955–1965	3.2	6.2
1965–1975	3.6	5.6
1975–1980	.9	3.1

Oil consumption: 1945–1965, Bureau of the Census, *Historical Statistics of the United States* (Washington, D.C.: U.S. Government Printing Office, 1975), Part 2, Series S-19, p. 818; 1965–1980, Bureau of the Census, *Statistical Abstract of the United States 1981* (Washington, D.C.: U.S. Government Printing Office, 1981), p. 734. Electric consumption: 1945–1965, *Historical Statistics,* Part 2, Series S-120, p. 828; 1965–1980, *Statistical Abstract,* p. 587. The decade 1962–1972 provides a more startling contrast with both prior and subsequent growth rates in each series. However, this choice of dates could be criticized as arbitrary and manipulative.

32   Zvi Griliches, "Research Expenditures, Education, and the Aggregate Agricultural Production Function," *The American Economic Review,* Vol. LIV, No. 6 (December 1964), pp. 968–69, calculates that $250 spent by farmers on additional fertilizer added $1267 to the value of output in 1949 and $697 in 1959. As a result the use of fertilizers had been and was continuing to increase very rapidly.

33   *Historical Statistics,* Part 1, pp. 223 and 593, for GNP deflator and crude oil prices, respectively.

33   One measure of the technical exhaustion of the electric power industry

that is independent of rising inflation, interest rates, and fuel costs is the amount of electricity actually generated with a given amount of fuel. In coal-fired plants, kilowatt hours per ton of coal increased steadily to a peak in 1961 and have since shown a persistent decline. The rate of increase was 3.2 percent a year from 1920 through 1961 and then *minus* .7 percent through 1980. The rapid growth of thermal efficiency in oil-fired generators also comes to a halt in 1961, although modest growth is resumed in the 1970s. Kilowatt hours per barrel of oil increase at 3 percent a year from 1920 through 1961; and then grow at only .3 percent a year through 1980. Coal accounts for more than half, and coal plus oil for more than 70 percent of all U.S. electricity generation in both 1961 and 1980. *Historical Statistics,* Part 2, Series S-104 and S-105, p. 826; and *Statistical Abstract,* p. 587.

33   The average ¢ price paid by all users of electricity was 1.69¢ per kwh in 1960 and 1.59¢ in 1970, *Historical Statistics,* Part 2, Series S-119, p. 827.

34–   From 1960 to 1974 output of electricity grew by 6.1 percent a year and
35   installed generating capacity by 7.1 percent a year, *Statistical Abstract,* p. 587. At the same time, the real GNP was growing by 3.8 percent a year, *The Economic Report of the President* (Washington, D.C.: U.S. Government Printing Office, 1982), p. 234. Plant and equipment spending by electric utilities and by all U.S. businesses is reported on a quarterly basis in U.S. Department of Commerce, *Survey of Current Business* (Washington, D.C.: U.S. Government Printing Office), Vol. 55, No. 3 (March 1975), p. S-2, as well as on the same page of every other monthly issue. The ratios of real, private, nonresidential investment to real GNP are calculated from *Economic Report of the President,* 1982, p. 234; and Bert G. Hickman and Robert M. Coen, *An Annual Growth Model of the U.S. Economy* (Amsterdam/New York/Oxford: North-Holland Publishing Co., 1976), p. 221. Corporate cash flow as a percentage of GNP is given in *Economic Report of the President,* 1982, p. 333. Sources of funds for corporate capital spending, *ibid.,* p. 334.

35   Inflation rates for 1965–1974, *ibid.,* p. 237.

35–   Military spending, GNP and Gross Private Domestic Investment in 1965
36   and 1974, *ibid.* p. 233; transfer payments, *ibid.,* p. 321. Corporate and federal debts for the same years are from *The Survey of Current Business,* Vol. 50, No. 5 (May 1970), p. 14; and Vol. 55, No. 7 (July 1975), p. 10.

36   The best single measure of "the pressure of production on capacity" should be the ratio of actual, real GNP to potential GNP, *Survey of Current Business,* Vol. 60, No. 11 (November 1980), p. 17. I have relied also on the Federal Reserve Board's measure of capacity utilization in manufacturing to verify my statement, *Economic Report of the President,* 1982, p. 283.

36   In 1974 the Implicit Price Deflator for GNP, the broadest available index of inflation, was 58 percent higher than it had been in 1964. The price

index for Personal Consumption was higher by 53 percent; for fixed Gross Private Domestic Investment prices had advanced by 60 percent; while for investment in nonresidential structures (including electric power plants) prices had gone up by 97.5 percent, *Economic Report of the President*, 1982, p. 236.

36 Jordan D. Lewis, "Technology, Enterprise, and American Economic Growth," *Science*, Vol. 215 (March 1982), pp. 1206–7. This portion of Lewis's provocative essay draws upon and quotes from a study by W. J. Abernathy and R. S. Rosenbloom in *Policy Outlook: Science, Technology, and the Issues of the Eighties* (Washington, D.C.: American Association for the Advancement of Science, 1981).

CHAPTER 5

38 Inflation and unemployment data from *Economic Report of the President* (Washington, D. C.: U.S. Government Printing Office, 1982), pp. 236 and 271, respectively. For productivity, *ibid.*, pp. 278–79 and Edward F. Denison, *Accounting for Slower Growth: The United States in the 1970's* (Washington, D.C.: Brookings Institution, 1980).

39 World petroleum prices are available from various issues of *Petroleum Intelligence Weekly* or *Platt's Oilgram*. Total U.S. energy prices are from the series "Fuels and related products, and power" in *Economic Report of the President*, 1982, p. 300. Total U.S. energy consumption in 1973 was 74.6 quads (a quad equals one quadrillion [10^{15}] BTU's), *Statistical Abstract of the United States 1981*, p. 582. In 1975 the estimated average cost of energy was $1.00 per million BTU's. I have taken the 1973 cost at $1 times the ratio of the "Fuel and related products" indices for 1973 and 1975. This indicates total 1973 energy expenditures of $40 billion, or 3 percent of a $1,326.4 billion GNP; see Denison, *Accounting for Slower Growth*, p. 138; Gordon J. MacDonald, "Long-Term Availability of Natural Resources," in *Alternatives for Growth*, Harvey J. McMains and Lyle Wilcox, eds. (New York: National Bureau of Economic Research, 1978), pp. 50–51.

40 For real hourly earnings in the nonfarm economy, see *Economic Report of the President*, 1982, p. 276; and *Survey of Current Business*, Vol. 62, No. 8 (August 1982), p. S-14.

40– For rates of productivity growth, see *Economic Report of the President*,
41 1982, p. 278; Denison, *Accounting for Slower Growth*, pp. 2, 94. For the growth of dollar wage rates, see the sources cited in the previous note.

42 The current dollar value of the net stocks of fixed, private, residential and nonresidential capital, plus government capital, all at the end of 1973, has been taken from *Survey of Current Business*, Vol. 61, No. 2 (February 1981), pp. 58, 62, 65. This figure was divided by GNP and Gross Private Domestic Investment for 1973, from *Economic Report of*

the President, 1982, p. 233. Strictly speaking, the number of years required to replace the entire capital stock (with no growth) could be more reasonably estimated by adding an estimate of government capital expenditures to Gross Private Domestic Investment in the denominator or by removing the government-owned portion of capital from the numerator. The latter technique leaves just over $2.1 trillion divided by $229.8 billion, or just over nine years at 1973's high rate of investment.

44   Suppose Profit Maximizing's airplane has a capacity of 200 passengers, costs $8,000 a day to own and uses 4,000 gallons of fuel on each flight. Profit Maximizing has 20 employees who are required whatever the number of daily flights, and another 20 for whom the need increases or decreases proportionately as the number of daily flights goes up or down from 10. Here is the initial situation:

Quantity per day	×	Price or Cost per item (per day)	=	Daily Revenue, or Cost
10 flights × 200 seats × 60% full = 1,200 passengers		$27 ticket price		$32,400 total revenue
40,000 gallons fuel		40¢ per gallon		16,000
20 people		$125 per day		2,500
20 people		$125 per day		2,500
1 airplane		$8,000 per day		8,000
				$29,000 total cost
				$3,400 daily profit before taxes (revenue minus cost)

And here is a table of Profit Maximizing's daily activity after the price of fuel has doubled and the airline has had a chance to adjust its schedule to only six flights a day and the price of a ticket to $33 instead of $27:

Quantity per day	×	Price or Cost per item (per day)	=	Daily Revenue, or Cost
6 flights × 200 seats × 80% full = 960 passengers		$33 ticket price		$31,680 total revenue

Quantity per day	×	Price or Cost per item (per day)	=	Daily Revenue, or Cost
24,000 gallons fuel		80¢ per gallon		19,200
12 people		$125 per day		1,500
20 people		$125 per day		2,500
1 airplane		$8,000 per day		8,000

$31,200 total cost
$480 daily profit
before taxes
(revenue
minus cost)

The reader should satisfy himself that, even if the same 1,200 passengers were willing to purchase tickets under the old ten-flight schedule at the new $33 price, Profit Maximizing would lose money, with daily revenue of $39,600 and expenses of $45,000. The numbers in this example are representative of what actually happened to the airline industry after 1973; but they are not exact in either magnitude or proportion.

Notice that output (passenger flights) per worker goes from 1,200/40 to 960/32. That is, it is unchanged at 30. Output per unit of capital (one airplane) declines exactly 20 percent from 1,200 to 960. "Total factor productivity" is the ratio of output to a combined value for labor and capital used. The inputs are usually combined by using their dollar prices. Since prices for labor and capital don't change in my example, total factor productivity is simply the ratio of passenger flights to the sum of labor and airplane costs. This measure declines by 13⅓ percent from 1200/13,000 to 960/12,000.

45   If the entire capital stock from dams to dishwashers depreciates at the rate of 2 percent a year (loses half its value in about 35 years), while investment in new facilities proceeds at a rate sufficient to relace this depreciation and increase the net capital stock by 2.5 percent a year, then the amount of time required for any existing stock of capital to become only half of the enlarged stock as a result of depreciation and growth is the solution for n in the equation $(.98/1.025)^n = .5$. That solution is $n = 15.4$ years. Hence, if all investment after 1973 reflected the new relative price of energy, half the nation's capital stock would finally do so in 1988. If the 1978–80 OPEC price shocks required further capital modification, these would not influence half the capital stock until the mid- or late 1990s. The estimate of 10 to 12 years in the case of private plant and equipment is based on a net growth rate of 3 percent a year and a depreciation rate of 2.5 percent to 3 percent a year (half worn out in about 25 years). See the sources cited for page 42.

45   It is reasonable to suppose that the loss of productivity growth after 1973 was about 2 percent a year or more, based on the sources in the note for pages 40–41.

46 *Economic Report of the President*, 1982, p. 333, for the stock market valuation of corporate assets.

46 On the composition of recent investment spending, see Goldman Sachs, *The Pocket Chartroom*, October 1981, pp. 1g, 1h.

47 The values of U.S. petroleum products imports and merchandise imports and exports with OPEC countries are in *Economic Report of the President*, 1982, pp. 348–49. Average GNP and average federal deficits from *ibid.*, pp. 233, 318.

48 Inflation and unemployment, *Economic Report of the President*, 1982, pp. 237, 269.

49 This analysis of the changing composition of investment is from the source given for page 46.

51 In the spring of 1982, a barrel of proven oil beneath deep northern waters, such as Georges Bank, had a market value of about $6; long-term U.S. government bonds yielded about 13.5 percent; and many people would have agreed that 5 percent a year was a reasonable estimate of the rate at which fish prices would increase for the indefinite future. Accordingly, 5 billion barrels of oil beneath Georges Bank had a market value of $30 billion dollars. At 17 million barrels a day, 5 billion barrels would last the United States for 294 days. I estimate the value of an annual fish catch on Georges Bank at $2 billion (2 billion pounds at an average $1 a pound to the fishermen). The present value of that catch, sustained forever, was $2 billion $\times \sum_{i=0}^{\infty} (1.05/1.135)^i = \$26.7$ billion. The fish that were so valued are approximately enough to supply all of the protein requirements of 11 million people for all time. Whether or not these particular estimates of oil reserves and fish harvests are correct, they accurately juxtapose the logic of the price system against human sensibility.

CHAPTER 6

54– For a brief synopsis of the 1948 General Motors agreement, see "The '82
55 Auto Negotiations: Last Hurrah?" *Wall Street Journal*, December 3, 1981, p. 28; or any standard labor history.

55 Growth rates for labor productivity in 9 major categories (manufacturing, services, etc.) and 40 more specific industries from 1948 through 1966, are given in John W. Kendrick, *Postwar Productivity Trends in the United States, 1948–1969* (New York: Columbia University Press, 1973), pp. 94–95.

56 *Economic Report of the President* (Washington, D.C.: U.S. Government Printing Office, 1982), pp. 237, 278, 310, for inflation, wages, and interest rates, respectively.

58 For the aggregate operating statement of the nonfinancial corporate sector, see any recent issue of *Survey of Current Business*, Table 1.13.

59   Labor union membership, Bureau of the Census, *Statistical Abstract of the United States, 1981* (Washington, D.C.: U.S. Government Printing Office, 1981), pp. 411–12.

60   John Maynard Keynes, *A Tract on Monetary Reform* (London: Macmillan, 1971), p. 148.

61   Arthur M. Okun, *Prices and Quantities* (Washington, D.C.: The Brookings Institution, 1981), pp. 279, 283. The book was published posthumously. The date of the quote is 1980, before we were deprived of Okun's understanding and wit. Although I have developed many of the ideas in this chapter for over a decade, my presentation here owes much to Okun's work, which is a masterful survey of the theory of actual price behavior and inertia in the contemporary economy.

CHAPTER 7

62   George L. Perry, "Inflation in Theory and Practice," *Brookings Papers on Economic Activity*, 1:1980, p. 215; Arthur M. Okun, *Prices and Quantities* (Washington, D.C.: The Brookings Institution, 1981), p. 282.

65   The 1983 budget of the United States envisions payments of $197.215 billion to Social Security, Railroad Retirement, and federal employee beneficiaries. This sum is estimated to grow at a rate of 7.9 percent a year from 1981 through 1985. This would be a reasonable projection further into the future on the assumption that the population of beneficiaries will grow about 1.8 percent a year and the level of benefits about 6 percent a year (*Budget of the United States Government: Fiscal Year 1983* [Washington, D.C.: U.S. Government Printing Office, 1982], p. 5-143). The present value of $197.215 billion, growing at 7.9 percent a year for 65 years and discounted at a long-term U.S. Government bond interest rate of 10.5 percent, is 6.6 trillion. The face amount of the federal government's debt at this writing is just over $1 trillion; its market value, with bonds yielding 10.5 percent, is somewhat less. At the end of 1982, the face amount of all outstanding American indebtedness was approximately $4.8 trillion (compare with Henry Kaufman, *1982 Prospects for Financial Markets* [New York: Salomon Brothers, Inc., 1982], p. 20). Again, the market value of this debt, most of which was issued at lower interest rates, was less than its face amount.

65   For a more comprehensive statement of the ill effects that Social Security taxes have upon both unemployment and inflation, see Robert Eisner, "Employment Taxes and Subsidies," *Hearings Before the Task Force on Inflation of the Committee on the Budget, House of Representatives*, Vol. 2, 96th Congress, First Session, 1979, pp. 408–12; and, by the same author, "A Way to Create Jobs: Cut Payroll Taxes," *New York Times*, August 17, 1975, reproduced on p. 448 of the same volume of hearings.

PART II

CHAPTER 8

71   Arthur Cecil Pigou, *The Veil of Money* (Toronto, Canada: Macmillan, 1949).

72–   For two expertly informed, but mercifully readable, accounts of trading
73   more than 11,000 and much more than 35,000 years ago see (respectively) Jane Jacobs, *The Economy of Cities* (New York: Vintage Books, 1970), pp. 18–36; and Bjorn Kurten, *Dance of the Tiger* (New York: Pantheon, 1980).

75   Richard Duncan-Jones, *The Economy of the Roman Empire* (Cambridge: Cambridge University Press, 1974), Parts 1 and 2.

75–   There is a vast and often contentious literature on the development of
77   money and banking in the European Dark and Middle Ages. Important general accounts are contained in Robert-Henri Bautier, *The Economic Development of Medieval Europe* (New York: Harcourt Brace Jovanovich, 1971); Robert S. Lopez, *The Commercial Revolution of the Middle Ages, 950–1350* (Cambridge: Cambridge University Press, 1976); Henri Pirenne, *Economic and Social History of Medieval Europe* (New York: Harcourt, Brace & World [1962], first published in 1933).

79   Seminal studies that led to an appreciation of the importance of intangible human skills include Theodore W. Schultz, "Capital Formation by Education," *Journal of Political Economy*, December 1960, pp. 571–83; Robert M. Solow, "Technical Change and the Aggregate Production Function," *Review of Economics and Statistics*, Vol. 39, No. 3 (August 1957), pp. 312–20; Edward F. Denison, *The Sources of Economic Growth in the United States* (New York: Committee for Economic Development, 1962); and Gary S. Becker, *Human Capital* (New York: National Bureau of Economic Research, 1964).

79   For a description of medieval accomplishments see the works cited above for pp. 75–77, and more particularly Lynn White, Jr., *Medieval Technology and Social Change* (Oxford: Oxford University Press, 1962).

79   On prices and bullion in the twelfth to fourteenth centuries, see Lopez, *The Commercial Revolution*, pp. 70–73.

80   Karl Marx, *Capital*, Vol. I (New York: International Publishers, 1967), p. 128.

80–   Benjamin Franklin, "The Nature and Necessity of a Paper-Currency,
81   1729," in *The Papers of Benjamin Franklin*, Vol. I, Leonard W. Labaree, ed. (New Haven: Yale University Press, 1959), p. 150.

82   John Hicks, *A Theory of Economic History* (Oxford: Oxford University Press, 1969), pp. 9–24. Peter Temin, "Modes of Behavior," *Journal of Economic Behavior and Organization*, Vol. I (1980), pp. 175–95, extends Hicks's Custom-Command-Market trichotomy into a rigorous theory of the relationship between these descriptions of institutional ar-

rangements and analogous triads of personality types and circumstantial stimuli.

Chapter 9

85   Adam Smith, *The Wealth of Nations,* Vol. I (London: J. M. Dent, 1964), pp. 257–58. John Adams, 1809, in Bray Hammond, *Banks and Politics in America from the Revolution to the Civil War* (Princeton: Princeton University Press, 1957), p. 196.

87–   This description of inflation during the Revolutionary War consists of
88   rough estimates from imprecise sources, including Arthur Harrison Cole, *Wholesale Commodity Prices in the United States, 1700–1861: Statistical Supplement* (Cambridge, Mass.: Harvard University Press, 1938); Bureau of the Census, *Historical Statistics of the United States* (Washington, D.C.: U.S. Government Printing Office, 1975), p. 52, Series E-52; Anne Bezanson, *Prices and Inflation During the American Revolution* (Philadelphia: University of Pennsylvania Press, 1951); Harold Underwood Faulkner, *American Economic History* (New York: Harper & Brothers, 1960), p. 138; Edward H. Phelps Brown and Sheila V. Hopkins, "Seven Centuries of the Price of Consumables, Compared with Builder's Wage Rates," *Economica,* Vol. 23 (1956); and the essay by Benjamin Franklin, cited below.

89   Benjamin Franklin, "The Paper Money of the United States" [1780?], reprinted in Guy Stevens Callender, *Selections from the Economic History of the United States, 1765–1860* (New York: Augustus M. Kelley, 1965), p. 143.

90   Thomas Jefferson, letter to Colonel Charles Yancey, January 6, 1816, in *The Life and Selected Writings of Thomas Jefferson,* Adrienne Koch and William Peden, eds. (New York: Random House, 1944), pp. 657–58.

90–   My discussion closely follows and is greatly indebted to the wonderful
92   narrative and analysis in Bray Hammond, *Banks and Politics in America.*

Chapter 10

93–   The factual story and the analysis in these pages is virtually all from
97   Milton Friedman and Anna Jacobson Schwartz, *A Monetary History of the United States, 1867–1960* (New York: National Bureau of Economic Research, 1963).

101   Friedman and Schwartz, *A Monetary History,* pp. 443–45. For loan to deposit ratios see Bureau of the Census, *Historical Statistics of the United States* (Washington, D.C.: U.S. Government Printing Office, 1975), Part 2, p. 1019; and after 1970, various issues of the Board of Governors of the Federal Reserve System, *Federal Reserve Bulletin,* Table 1.25, p. A 17.

102   For Eurodollar statistics through 1972, and an outstanding general dis-

cussion of the topic, Raymond F. Mikesell and J. Herbert Furth, *Foreign Dollar Balances and the International Role of the Dollar* (New York: National Bureau of Economic Research, 1974). For more recent Euro-dollar statistics, the table, "Eurocurrency market size," in any monthly issue of *World Financial Markets*, Morgan Guaranty Trust Co.

103–
04   The concentration of Eurobanking deposits, borrowings, and banks has been estimated from various issues of *World Financial Markets*, various *Annual Reports* of the Bank for International Settlements, and various *Fortune* magazine listings of the fifty largest financial institutions in the United States and in the rest of the world.

PART III
Chapter 11

111–
13   N. D. Kondratieff, "The Long Waves in Economic Life," *Review of Economic Statistics*, Vol. 18 (November 1935), pp. 105–15; George Garvy, "Kondratieff's Theory of Long Cycles," *Review of Economic Statistics*, Vol. 26 (November 1943), pp. 203–20; Joseph A. Schumpeter, *History of Economic Analysis* (Oxford: Oxford University Press, 1954), p. 743.

114   Geoffrey H. Moore and Julius Shiskin, *Indicators of Business Expansions and Contractions* (New York: National Bureau of Economic Research, 1967), p. 113; and Bureau of the Census; *Statistical Abstract of the United States, 1981* (Washington, D.C.: U.S. Government Printing Office, 1981), p. 549.

114–
15   Change in inventories and GNP, *Economic Report of the President* (Washington, D.C.: U.S. Government Printing Office, 1982), p. 240; the same data before 1929, John W. Kendrick, *Productivity Trends in the United States* (New York: Arno Press, 1975), pp. 296–97. Quarterly and monthly data on inventories and GNP or retail sales, along with a view that inventories are a prime mover of business cycles, can be found in Alan S. Blinder, "Retail Inventory Behavior and Business Fluctuations," *Brookings Papers on Economic Activity*, 2, 1981 (Washington, D.C.: The Brookings Institution, 1982), pp. 443–505. Consumer durables, *Economic Report of the President*, 1982, p. 248.

116   William D. Nordhaus, "The Political Business Cycle," *Review of Economic Studies*, Vol. 42 (1975).

116   On the timing of business cycles see the sources given above for page 114.

118   Residential construction, Bureau of the Census, *Historical Statistics of the United States*, Part 2 (Washington, D.C.: U.S. Government Printing Office, 1975), Series N 71,73, p. 623; *Economic Report of the President*, 1982, p. 235.

120–   Richard A. Easterlin, *Population, Labor Force, and Long Swings in Eco-*
21   *nomic Growth* (New York: National Bureau of Economic Research,
       1968).
121   William C. Freund, "The Looming Impact of Population Changes," *Wall
       Street Journal*, April 6, 1982, p. 35.

CHAPTER 12

124   W. W. Rostow, "Kondratieff, Schumpeter, and Kuznets: Trend Periods
       Revisted," *Journal of Economic History*, Vol. 35, No. 4 (December
       1975), pp. 719–753; Joseph A. Schumpeter, *Business Cycles*, 2 Vols.
       (New York: McGraw-Hill, 1939).
125   Nathan Rosenberg, *Perspectives on Technology* (Cambridge, Eng.: Cam-
       bridge University Press, 1976), pp. 250–51.
125   Rosenberg, *Perspectives on Technology*, pp. 251–53.
126–   Current wholesale prices from various issues of the *Wall Street Journal*.
27   For 1929 see Charles P. Kindleberger, *The World in Depression, 1929–
       1939* (Berkeley: University of California Press, 1973), pp. 87–89.
128   For U.S. automobiles in use, their age distribution and the number re-
       tired from use each year, Bureau of the Census, *Statistical Abstract of
       the United States* (Washington, D.C.: U.S. Government Printing Office,
       1981), pp. 620, 624. Persons fed per farmworker, Bureau of the Census,
       Historical Statistics of the United States, Part 1 (Washington, D.C.: U.S.
       Government Printing Office, 1975). Series K 407, p. 498; extrapolated
       from 1970 to 1980 from *Statistical Abstract of the United States*, 1981,
       p. 681.
129   John Maynard Keynes, *A Tract on Monetary Reform* (London: Macmil-
       lan, 1971), p. 65.

PART IV

CHAPTER 13

134   Kenneth J. Arrow, *Social Choice and Individual Values* (New York:
       John Wiley, 1951).
136   Friedrich A. Hayek, *The Road to Serfdom* (Chicago: The University of
       Chicago Press, 1957), p. xi.
138   The relationship between the degree of economic backwardness and the
       degree of resort to state intervention is developed by Alexander
       Gerschenkron, *Economic Backwardness in Historical Perspective* (Cam-
       bridge, Mass.: Harvard University Press, 1962).
140   John Maynard Keynes, *The General Theory of Employment, Interest,
       and Money*, Harcourt, Brace & World, 1964, p. 378.

CHAPTER 14

145 Anyone who thinks that confusion about the proper definition of money is a phenomenon caused by recent monetary innovations should read the 110-page Part One, "Definition of Money," in Milton Friedman and Anna Jacobson Schwartz, *Monetary Statistics of the United States* (New York: National Bureau of Economic Research, 1970), which follows their *Monetary History*. In this extensive discussion, the authors make no claim that there is anything like a "correct" definition of money or even firm limits on the range of correct definitions.

145 For the compromise view of the causes of the Depression (which monetarists vehemently reject) see Peter Temin, *Did Monetary Forces Cause the Great Depression?* (New York: W. W. Norton, 1976); the article by Robert J. Gordon and James A. Wilcox cited above in the note for page 6; and Robert B. Zevin, "The Economics of Normalcy," *Journal of Economic History*, Vol. 42, No. 1 (March 1982), pp. 43–52.

145 John Kenneth Galbraith, *The Affluent Society*, 3rd edition, revised (Boston: Houghton Mifflin Co., 1976), p. 179.

149 For a history of recent interest rate movements, see *Economic Report of the President* (Washington, D.C.: U.S. Government Printing Office, 1982), pp. 310–11; unemployment, *ibid.,* pp. 266–67.

150 Recent inflation rates, *ibid.,* p. 237. For recent money growth rates see various monthly issues of *Monetary Trends,* Federal Reserve Bank of St. Louis.

CHAPTER 15

154 Herbert Stein, "Do We Know What Reagan Economics Is?" *Wall Street Journal,* March 11, 1982, p. 37; John Brooks, "The Supply Side," *New Yorker,* April 19, 1982, p. 108.

156 Herbert Stein, *Wall Street Journal,* March 11, 1982.

157 For a succinct statement of the principles of supply side economics, see Arthur B. Laffer, "Supply-Side Economics," *Financial Analysts Journal,* September–October 1981, pp. 29–43.

157 Federal government expenditure breakdown, *The Economic Report of the President* (Washington, D.C.: U.S. Government Printing Office, 1982), p. 321.

159– John A. Tatom, "We Are All Supply-Siders Now!" *Review,* Vol. 63, No.
60   5 (May 1981), Federal Reserve Bank of St. Louis, pp. 18–30; *Economic Report of the President,* 1982, p. 266.

160 For the origins of the Laffer Curve, see John Brooks, "The Supply Side," p. 99, cited above for page 154.

162 For the history of total tax receipts and GNP, see *Economic Report of the President,* 1982, pp. 320 and 230, respectively.

163 Between 1960 and 1976, over half of all the net, new, private jobs in the

United States were created by firms with 20 or fewer employees, over 56 percent by firms with 50 or fewer employees, David L. Birch, *The Job Generation Process* (Cambridge, Mass.: MIT Program on Neighborhood and Regional Change, 1979), p. 30.

PART V

CHAPTER 16

174   For a more optimistic view of voluntary guidelines see Arthur M. Okun, *Prices and Quantities* (Washington, D.C.: The Brookings Institution, 1981), pp. 342–48.

174–   There is a large, disputatious literature on French indicative planning. A
75   balanced, middle view, which illuminates many of the shortcomings ignored in my brief description, is found in Stephen S. Cohen, *Modern Capitalist Planning: The French Model* (Berkeley: University of California Press, 1977).

175   Ibid., p. 10.

176   Let labor income = W × L, where W is the wage rate and L is hours of labor used. Total income = P × O, where P is the average price level and O is the volume of output. An unchanged share of labor income in total income (and therefore of property income in the total as well) means that $\dfrac{W \times L}{P \times O} = \dfrac{W' \times L'}{P' \times O'}$, where the symbol " ' " denotes wages, hours, prices or output after the passage of some time. This equation can be rearranged to show that $W'/W = P'/P \times \dfrac{O'/L'}{O/L}$, or the ratio of new wages to old wages equals the ratio of new prices to old prices times the ratio of new to old labor productivity.

177   *Economic Report of the President* (Washington, D.C.: U.S. Government Printing Office, 1982), p. 278.

178   Government sector relative employment and purchase of goods, *ibid.*, pp. 240, 266–67, 275, 321–22. Transfer payments, *ibid.*, pp. 321–22. Board of Governors of the Federal Reserve System, *The Quarterly Economic Model*, 1978, in the consumption equation (I.1), finds that consumption out of the sum of Federal and local transfer payments equals 100.41 percent of the value of the transfers. This is the most statistically significant relationship in the entire equation.

179   Federal transfers to local governments, *Economic Report of the President*, 1982, pp. 320–21.

CHAPTER 17

184   *Budget of the United States Government, Fiscal Year 1983* (Washington, D.C.: U.S. Government Printing Office, 1982), p. 4-10.

185 The tax cuts and present tax burdens affecting the top 4 percent of the income spectrum have been estimated from Kenneth H. Bacon, "The Outlook," *Wall Street Journal,* December 21, 1981, p. 1; *Budget of the U.S. Government, Fiscal 1983,* p. 4-2; *Statistical Abstract of the United States, 1981* (Washington, D.C.: U.S. Government Printing Office, 1981), pp. 259, 432.

185 For the relative importance of reductions in estate and corporate income taxes see the source cited for page 184.

186 For the increases in defense, net interest and other lines of the 1982 Federal budget, see *Economic Report of the President,* 1982 (Washington, D.C.: U.S. Government Printing Office, 1982), p. 317.

188 The ratio of two or a little less total increase in GNP for every additional one dollar independently spent by government was calculated by Keynes in 1936 in *The General Theory of Employment, Interest, and Money;* and by the Council of Economic Advisers in the 1962 *Economic Report of the President;* while I have calculated ratios ranging from slightly more than two at the beginning of this century to slightly less in the recent past, in "The Economics of Normalcy," *Journal of Economic History,* Vol. 42, No. 1 (March 1982), p. 49. The average 20 percent share of federal government receipts in GNP for the 1980s is calculated from *Economic Report of the President,* 1982, pp. 233, 317; thus yielding 40¢ out of every $2.00. The 1982 federal budget cost per person unemployed has been calculated as $4,650 from *Budget of the U.S. Government, Fiscal 1983,* pp. 2-13, 2-14. Average GNP per employed person in 1982 has been taken at $31,000 ($3.1 trillion divided by 100 million workers). Since $4,650 is exactly 15 percent of $31,000, the budget saving on a $2.00 increase in GNP, caused by a proportionate increase in employment, is 15 percent, or 30¢.

189 On the propensity of Social Security recipients to spend all of their benefits on consumption, see the note above for page 178.

190 An additional $100 billion of federal demand for output would create an additional $200 billion of GNP, which would employ about 6.5 million out of the 11.5 million persons unemployed at the time of this writing. See the note for page 188.

CHAPTER 18

193 Edward F. Denison, *The Sources of Economic Growth in the United States and the Alternatives Before Us* (New York: Committee for Economic Development, 1962), p. 270, and *Accounting for Slower Growth* (Washington, D.C.: Brookings Institution, 1979), p. 2.

193 John W. Kendrick, *The Formation and Stocks of Total Capital* (New York: National Bureau of Economic Research, 1976), pp. 118–23 (rates of return); p. 106 (investment in structures and equipment as well as education and training for 1929, 1948, and 1969); p. 239 (material to

calculate the ratio of intangible human investment to tangible, reproducible investment in 1973). The average and nearly constant growth of the ratio of human capital to tangible capital from 1929 to 1973 produces equality between the two magnitudes in 1983 or 1984 by simple extrapolation.

Index

Adams, John, 85, 86, 90, 92
Addictive rate of inflation, 62–64, 66, 170. *See also* "Embedded" rate of inflation; Inertia of inflation
Affluent Society, The (Galbraith), 26
American Business Council, and supply side economics, 163
Anti-inflationary policy, impact of, 47–48. *See also* Keynesian policies
Arrow, Kenneth, 134
"Automatic stabilizers," government spending shifts as, 19–20

Balance of payments, 101
Bank panics: and creation of money, 91–92; Eurodollar threat of, 102–106; and Federal Reserve System, 94; of 1929–33, 95
Banks: beginnings of, 76–77; Certificates of Deposit by, 98–99; foreclosure reluctance of, 63–64; as inflation losers, 66; and interest-rate regulation, 98, 100–101; and investment functions, 96, 97–98; money creation by, 11, 85–87; Money Market Deposit Accounts in, 100; Repurchase Agreements by, 99–100. *See also* Federal Reserve System
Bills of exchange, in origins of credit, 76–77
Bismarck, Otto von, 138
Borrowing: and demand, 203; and excess spending, 14; and inflation, 6–7, 30, 35–37, 63, 197–206; in monetarist theory, 146–47, 148; and money creation, 91–92; and security against depression, 17–18, 30.

See also Deficit spending; Investment
Bryan, William Jennings, 66, 91
Budget deficit. *See* Deficit, federal
Burns, Arthur, 156
Bush, George, 165
Business borrowing, and inflation, 30, 35, 36, 37
Business cycles, 113–116. *See also* Economic cycles

Capital, abstract aggregation of, 21–22, 23–24
Capital goods: and increased energy expense, 41–45, 211–212n; obsolescence of, 45–46; utilization of, 48. *See also* Durable goods
Carter administration: economic conflict in, 165; monetarism by, 149; wage-price guidelines by, 173, 179
Carter Energy Program, and electric rate reform, 33
Certificates of Deposit (CDs), 98–99
Chandler, Lester V., 181
Changing Roles of Debt and Equity in Financing U.S. Capital Formation, The (Friedman), 199
Chrysler Corporation, government protection of, 155
Classical economic theory: Keynesian critique of, 24, 140–41; perfect competition in, 24. *See also* Conservative economics
Coinage, first appearance of, 74–75
Commercial Crises and Their Periodic Recurrence in France, in England, and in America (Juglar), 116

223